CARMELITE BIBLE MEDITATIONS
Saint Albert's Press

The Gospel Sustains Me

The word of God in the life and love of Saint Thérèse of Lisieux

LAUS DEO SEMPER ET MARIAE

THE GOSPEL SUSTAINS ME

*The word of God in the life and
love of Saint Thérèse of Lisieux*

EDITED BY JOHAN BERGSTRÖM-ALLEN, T.O.C.
& WILFRID McGREAL, O.CARM.

Saint Albert's Press & Edizioni Carmelitane
2009

First published 2009 by Saint Albert's Press & Edizioni Carmelitane.

Saint Albert's Press
Whitefriars, 35 Tanners Street,
Faversham, Kent, ME13 7JN, United Kingdom
www.carmelite.org
ISBN-10: 0-904849-40-6
ISBN-13: 978-0-904849-40-0

Edizioni Carmelitane
Centro Internationale S. Alberto
Via Sforza Pallavicini, 10
00193 Roma, Italy
www.carmelites.info/edizioni
ISBN-13: 978-88-7288-106-4

Designed by Johan Bergström-Allen, Carmelite Projects & Publications Office, York.

Typeset by Ing. Jakub Kubů, Prague, Czech Republic, on behalf of Karmelitánské nakladatelství s.r.o., Thákurova 3, 160 00 Praha 6, Czech Republic.

Printed by ERMAT Praha s.r.o., Czech Republic.

Contents

Note on editions used and symbols denoting them

Works by Thérèse of Lisieux

LC   *St. Thérèse of Lisieux: Her Last Conversations*, trans. John Clarke, O.C.D., (Washington, D.C.: I.C.S. Publications, 1977).

LT   *Letters of St. Thérèse: General Correspondence*, 2 volumes, trans. John Clarke, O.C.D., (Washington, D.C.: I.C.S. Publications, 1982 & 1988).

PN   *The Poetry of Saint Thérèse of Lisieux*, trans. Donald Kinney, O.C.D., (Washington, D.C.: I.C.S. Publications, 1996).

Pri   *The Prayers of Saint Thérèse of Lisieux*, trans. Aletheia Kane, O.C.D., (Washington, D.C.: I.C.S. Publications, 1997).

SS   *Story of a Soul: The Autobiography of Saint Thérèse of Lisieux*, trans. John Clarke, O.C.D., (Washington, D.C.: I.C.S. Publications, 1996).

Books of the Bible *in biblical order*

Genesis	Gn	Judith	Jdt
Exodus	Ex	Esther	Est
Leviticus	Lv	1 Maccabees	1 M
Numbers	Nb	2 Maccabees	2 M
Deuteronomy	Dt	Job	Jb
Joshua	Jos	Psalms	Ps
Judges	Jg	Proverbs	Pr
Ruth	Rt	Ecclesiastes	Qo
1 Samuel	1 S	Song of Songs	Sg
2 Samuel	2 S	Wisdom	Wis
1 Kings	1 K	Ecclesiasticus	Si
2 Kings	2 K	Isaiah	Is
1 Chronicles	1 Ch	Jeremiah	Jr
2 Chronicles	2 Ch	Lamentations	Lm
Ezra	Ezr	Baruch	Ba
Nehemiah	Ne	Ezekiel	Ezk
Tobit	Tb	Daniel	Dn

Hosea	Hos	Ephesians	Ep
Joel	Jl	Philippians	Ph
Amos	Am	Colossians	Col
Obadiah	Ob	1 Thessalonians	1 Th
Jonah	Jon	2 Thessalonians	2 Th
Micah	Mi	1 Timothy	1 Tm
Nahum	Na	2 Timothy	2 Tm
Habakkuk	Hab	Titus	Tt
Zephaniah	Zp	Philemon	Phm
Haggai	Hg	Hebrews	Heb
Zechariah	Zc	James	Jm
Malachi	Ml	1 Peter	1 P
Matthew	Mt	2 Peter	2 P
Mark	Mk	1 John	1 Jn
Luke	Lk	2 John	2 Jn
John	Jn	3 John	3 Jn
Acts	Ac	Jude	Jude
Romans	Rm	Revelation	Rv
1 Corinthians	1 Cor		
2 Corinthians	2 Cor		
Galatians	Ga		

... all books left me in aridity and I'm still in that state ... In this helplessness, Holy Scripture and The Imitation of Christ come to my aid; in them I discover a solid and very <u>pure</u> nourishment. But it is especially the <u>Gospels</u> which sustain me during my hours of prayer, for in them I find what is necessary for my poor little soul. I am constantly discovering in them new lights, hidden and mysterious meanings.

Saint Thérèse of Lisieux, Story of a Soul, *Manuscript A, Chapter VIII*

Foreword by the Dean of York Minster

St Thérèse has become deeply valued and loved by innumerable people both within the Roman Catholic Church and beyond. This is of a piece with the paradox of her whole life. On the surface her life was a withdrawal, a career in obscurity and seemingly without significance in the wider world. But this same Thérèse seems to us now of huge importance to our world, a major element in God's mission in our time. The journeying of her physical body in the form of her relics expresses this powerfully. She, for whom the loving mission of God was central, now literally embodies the direct approach of God to those who are far away, apparently on the edge.

This is how it will feel for us at York Minster when we welcome her relics on her feast day, 1ˢᵗ October 2009. People of every Christian tradition, and people of no allegiance, and even of no faith, pour through this place every day. And there we shall join in prayer to God that He will find His way, through Thérèse's prayers and witness, to draw everyone to Himself, so that we may all see Him face to face and be united in His love. This is surely how Thérèse has always wanted it to be: her prayer and longing attracts her, like her Lord, beyond the expected borders, to the outsider, even to the lost.

Keith Jones
Dean of York

A statue of Thérèse at Whitefriars Carmelite community in More House, York, England.

Preface by the editors

Thérèse of Lisieux is one of the best-loved saints within and beyond the Roman Catholic Church, and she is undoubtedly one of the 'superstars' of her religious family, the Carmelites, who have published this book to make her message better known. Her message is essentially that of the Gospel, the Good News, of Jesus Christ, which sustained Thérèse in times of happiness and sadness, light and dark.

Thérèse's appeal lies in the fact that she is able to point people simply, authentically, and directly to Jesus Christ, the Son of God. Her confidence and trust in God in all circumstances gives us hope and encouragement on our own faith journey. If we will let it, the relationship Thérèse had – and still has – with Jesus can inspire us to live more closely with him, and her evident closeness to Christ assures us that she's able to intercede with him on our behalf.

Thérèse is a model for Christians – and indeed for all people of good will – to follow, because she took to heart the words of the early Bible translator Saint Jerome: "Ignorance of Scripture is ignorance of Christ". What this publication hopes to do is to encourage people not only to know Thérèse better, but more importantly, to help them get to know better the Jesus that she loves so much.

Many books have been written about Thérèse, a selection of which you will find listed at the end of this publication along with other resources that might help you to know Jesus better through the experience of Carmelite spirituality.

This book begins with a very brief biography of Thérèse but does not attempt to give her complete life-story or summarise her spirituality; it is best, perhaps, to encounter that by reading her own autobiography, *Story of a Soul*, as well as her poetry, plays, and the transcripts of her last conversations. Rather, this publication is about the love that Thérèse of Lisieux had for another book, the Bible, and the God that she encountered in its pages. This is the subject that Alexander Vella introduces for us in his chapter. In an age when access to the Bible in one's own language wasn't common, Thérèse carried a copy of the Gospels next to her heart, and she must surely be delighted to think that her story might inspire us to do the same.

The chapter by Johan Bergström-Allen and Hugh Clarke sets Thérèse's love of the Bible in the context of Carmelite spirituality, which repeatedly emphasises the importance of Holy Scripture in the Christian life. The chapter is followed by a modern translation by Chris O'Donnell of the *Rule of Saint Albert*, the 'vision statement' of the Carmelite Family, which Thérèse, as a Carmelite nun, would have known well.

The chapter by Wilfrid McGreal highlights the important role that the Bible – especially the writings of Saint Paul – had in helping Thérèse to discern her vocation within the Church. It seems appropriate that this book is being published on the feast of the Conversion of Saint Paul in 2009, in the year designated by Pope Benedict XVI as a special 'Year of Saint Paul'. A reading of the *Rule of Saint Albert* shows just how important Paul is to Carmelites, both as a teacher and a model of faith.

Like all the saints, Thérèse wishes only to point her fellow Christians towards Christ. Her spiritual wisdom simply points us back to the Gospel, and this is the focus of the article which Joseph Chalmers and Camilo Maccise wrote as a joint letter when they served as Prior General and Superior General of the Ancient and Discalced branches of the Carmelite Family.

The chapter by James McCaffrey reveals how Thérèse gently draws us into an intimate friendship with the Jesus of the gospel accounts who is 'gentle and humble of heart' (*Matthew* 11:29), a Saviour eminently human, weak and vulnerable, revealing the heart of a God of mercy who is himself in need of our love. Thérèse also reminds us of the fragile nature of the Church, which is this same Christ spread out in the world.

Thérèse said towards the end of her short life that spiritual reading – even the most beautiful and touching – left her feeling dry and unmoved. The only text that spoke to her heart in this period of darkness and doubt were the Gospel accounts of Jesus' life. Even better than reading Thérèse's own words and the books about her is reading the word of God in the Bible. If you feel inspired to put this book down at any point and pick up the Scriptures instead, then this publication will have fulfilled its purpose.

In case you need some help and encouragement to take the Bible in hand, simple and useful guidance is offered by Joseph Chalmers in the chapter on *Lectio Divina*. This is followed by some excerpts from the writings of Thérèse juxtaposed with Bible passages that she quoted from; these might help you reflect on the word of God in your own life. You might first like to offer a short prayer asking Thérèse, Christ's 'Little Flower', to help and accompany you as you delve into the word of God which is 'living and active, sharper than any two-edged sword' (*Hebrews* 4:12).

The immediate impetus for this book is the visit of the relics of Saint Thérèse to England and Wales in September-October 2009, and we are delighted that – like the tour – this book draws on the contributions of Carmelites of both the Ancient Observance and the Discalced Reform. One of the highlights of the tour will be the visit to York Minster, the only non-Roman Catholic venue to host the relics. The fact that Thérèse's relics will be brought to a place of Anglican

St. Thérèse depicted in wood at the cathedral in the Belgian city of Ieper, which was largely destroyed during the First World War. Several soldiers and civilians spoke of Thérèse as a source of hope during the conflict, and attested to her intercession.

Louis and Zélie Martin, the parents of Saint Thérèse, beatified in 2008.

worship highlights the place of affection that many non-Roman Catholics have for the *Little Flower*. It is hoped that this booklet will help people of all faith backgrounds and none to come to better know Jesus of Nazareth, as seen through the eyes and the heart of his 'little Thérèse'. That would be her wish. As mentioned above, this book is being published on the feast of the Conversion of Saint Paul, which also marks the end of the Week of Prayer for Christian Unity. We hope and pray that in the years to come the communion of saints that is the Church will grow closer in bonds of love, united by our love of God's word.

As we welcome the relics of Thérèse across England and Wales, let us reflect on the words that the Little Flower jotted down at the top of one of her poems; they are words which Christ reputedly addressed to Saint Gertrude, and which surely apply to today's Christian as well:

> My daughter, seek those words of mine which most exude love. Write them down, and then, keeping them preciously like relics, take care to reread them often. When a friend wishes to reawaken the original vigour of his affection in the heart of his friend, he tells him:

'Remember what you felt in your heart when I said such and such a word,' or 'Do you remember your feelings at such a time, on such a day, in such a place?'... Be assured then that the most precious relics of mine on earth are my words of love, the words which have come from my most sweet Heart.[1]

Johan Bergström-Allen & Wilfrid McGreal
The Feast of the Conversion of Saint Paul
25th January 2009

Thérèse aged three and a half years old.

---

1   *The Life and Revelations of Saint Gertrude*, (Westminster: Christian Classics, 1983), p. 460.

Thérèse among other holy women of Carmel, depicted in ceramic by Adam Kossowski at The Friars, Aylesford, England.

A brief biography of Saint Thérèse

The remarkable woman we now know as Saint Thérèse, the 'Little Flower', was born Thérèse Martin in Alençon, France, on 2nd January 1873. When she was aged just four years old her mother Zélie died, and she moved to the Normandy town of Lisieux with her father Louis, a watchmaker, and her sisters. Three of those sisters – Marie, Pauline and Céline – entered the monastery of Carmelite nuns in Lisieux, and a fourth sister, Léonie, later became a Visitation nun.

Thérèse aged thirteen.

Though raised with the comforts of a bourgeois household, Thérèse was not always a happy child, particularly due to the death of her mother and the gradual separation from her sisters as they entered religious life. On Christmas night in 1886 Thérèse had a powerful experience of the love of God and resolved to make a new more positive beginning. She felt strongly called by God to join her sisters in the Carmel monastery, even asking the Pope for permission to enter despite her young age. The Bishop of Lisieux finally relented and allowed her to enter the community aged 15. She took the religious name of Sister Thérèse of the Child Jesus and the Holy Face.

In 1894 her father Louis died, and Thérèse herself became increasingly aware of the tuberculosis that would shortly take her own life. In January 1895, at the request of her sister Pauline, Thérèse began writing her autobiography, a collection of childhood reminiscences and accounts of her life in the monastery that together with some other writings was given the title *Story of a Soul*. More than simply a piece of nostalgia, *Story of a Soul* gave Thérèse the opportunity to describe her profound relationship with God, and to 'sing eternally the mercies of the Lord'.

Lisieux Carmel.

Thérèse died on 30th September 1897, aged just 24. A year after her death *Story of a Soul* was circulated and quickly gained a wide readership thanks to its author's frank and lively account of her relationship with God.

In her short life Thérèse achieved few great acts in the conventional sense; though her book is a best-seller she never set out to be an author, and though she is patron saint of the missions she never set foot on mission territory. Yet she realised in a simple and profound way that even small acts done out of love have great value in the sight of God. She called this insight the 'Little Way of Spiritual Childhood', regarding herself as a child who could trust and depend entirely on God's love for her. She also perceived the merciful nature of God, and in a sceptical age marked by harsh asceticism, Thérèse emphasised the love and the gentleness of God who she appreciated as Mother as well as Father.

Thérèse as a novice in 1889.

Thérèse is also revered for her confidence; despite great opposition she always strove to follow her dreams and her desire for God. She didn't always find life or her relationship with God and other people easy, but she spoke frankly and openly about her experiences, with which many people can identify. Thérèse wanted to do great things to preach the Good News of Jesus, but realised that she could not achieve these things by herself; she realised that God does great things through those who let God act in them. She realised that her vocation was to be 'love in the heart of the Church', having read the letters of Saint Paul. It was through reading such extracts from the Bible that Thérèse came to be nourished by the Word of God.

Thérèse realised the link between a love for the Bible, and a love for the God who inspired its books. Thérèse found that in reading the Gospel accounts of the life of Jesus Christ, she could draw closer and closer to him in the here and now. A century after her death, Pope John Paul II said: 'The real greatness of Thérèse of Lisieux is that, through her, we have discovered once again the simplicity and freshness of the gospel, which has its origin and source in the heart of Christ.'

In 1925 Thérèse was canonised a saint. In 1927 she was declared patron saint of the missions. In 1944 she was made one of the patron saints of France, and in 1997 she was declared a Doctor of the Church because her simple teaching is regarded as having universal significance for all followers of Jesus Christ.

Today over two million pilgrims visit Lisieux each year, as well as numerous shrines of Saint Thérèse around the world (details of some of which can be found at the end of this book). As well as being a marvellous model of how to live in allegiance to Jesus Christ, many people attest to her intercessory power with him. The miracles and graces that are granted through the intercession of Saint Thérèse are referred to as her 'shower of roses', since she predicted

The Basilica of Saint Thérèse in Lisieux.

herself that her real work of serving Christ and his followers would begin once she entered heaven.

Since the 1990s the mortal remains of Saint Thérèse have toured the world, and the visit of her relics has given people the opportunity to reflect on her message, which is simply a call back to the Good News of Jesus Christ that Thérèse discovered in the Scriptures.

*Statute of Saint Thérèse by Michael Clark
in the Great Courtyard at The Friars, Aylesford, England.*

A chasuble painted by St. Thérèse; the lilies represent her family, the closed lilies representing her brothers and sisters who had died.

The Bible in the life and in the writings of St. Thérèse of the Child Jesus

Alexander Vella, O.Carm.

One of the things which impressed the Carmelites of Lisieux in their young Sister Thérèse of the Child Jesus was her love for the Bible and her knowledge of it.

We have not had the privilege of living with Thérèse of Lisieux and listening to her conversations. We know her only through her writings and what her contemporaries recalled about her after her death in 1897. But these are enough to show us how much Thérèse was imbued with Holy Scripture. We find in her writings more than a thousand biblical quotations, besides very many allusions to biblical texts. Quite often in her works Thérèse does not simply quote a Bible passage, but dwells on it for quite a while, sometimes even commenting on it word by word. For us today this love for the word of God is considered only normal in someone who is taking his or her Christian faith seriously, but it was not so in Thérèse's time.

The sources of Thérèse's biblical knowledge

The time when Thérèse of Lisieux lived – the second half of the nineteenth century – did not favour the reading of the Bible. Some Old Testament passages which were considered to be 'indecent' could not be read, and you were looked upon with suspicion if you had a copy of the whole Bible among your books (because it was sometimes seen as an indication that you were seeking theological understanding outside the supervision of the Church). It is very probable that a copy of the entire Bible was never available to Thérèse. Her uncle, Isidore Guerin, had two copies of the Bible in his library, and after Thérèse's entrance into 'Carmel' (the Carmelite monastery of nuns), her sister Céline consulted those books and copied some passages from them. But Thérèse had been too young when she entered Carmel and she would not have been allowed to consult the Bible herself.

In the library of the Carmel of Lisieux there was a French translation of the Bible that, however, did not contain all the books of Holy Scripture; only the prioress, the sub-prioress and the librarian could consult it. The other nuns had to ask the permission of the prioress – and the novices also that of their mother mistress – to borrow a book from the library.

23

There was, however, a nun in the Carmel of Lisieux, Mother Coeur-de-Jésus (Heart of Jesus), who had a French translation of the Bible of her own; with the due permission of the prioress she could lend her Bible to the other nuns. Therefore Thérèse came to know the Bible not by reading the Bible itself, but by reading passages from it which she found in other books.

Besides the fact that it was a rare privilege to have a Bible of your own, we should also remember that the Liturgy in those days was all in Latin and therefore incomprehensible for the greatest part of the people, including Thérèse whose mother-tongue was French. Yet the Martin family used to gather in the evening to read a book by Dom Guéranger called *The Liturgical Year* which included a French translation of the biblical texts proclaimed in the liturgy. The same book was also read in the Lisieux Carmel, where they also had a French translation of the Breviary (the texts of the Divine Office).

In her childhood, Thérèse read various books of 'Sacred History' and a *Life of Jesus* from which she learned the principal events narrated in the Bible and picked-up some of the parables and sayings of Jesus. Avid as she was for the word of God, Thérèse used to look for biblical quotations in almanacs, liturgical books, lives of saints and holy pictures. She kept them in her mind and often quoted them. Two books that were her very dear to her in her youth were the medieval classic *The Imitation of Christ* by Thomas à Kempis, and a book by Abbé Arminjon entitled *The end of the present world and the mysteries of the future life*. Happily these books are full of biblical quotations.

In Carmel, besides the *Imitation of Christ*, Thérèse loved to read the works of the Spanish Carmelite friar St. John of the Cross in which she found an abundance of biblical quotations. When Céline entered Carmel, she brought with her a notebook in which she had copied passages from the Old Testament. Thérèse not only consulted it, but made a copy of it for herself. It was in this notebook that later on she would find the passages that constitute the biblical foundation of her 'Little Way'.

The only books of the Bible which Thérèse had for her own use were the four Gospel accounts: Matthew, Mark, Luke and John. Originally they were part of a book entitled *Manual of the Christian*, but Thérèse tore them from the *Manual* and bound them as a small book which she always carried on her heart.

Thérèse nourished by Holy Scripture

We have seen that already as a child Thérèse looked for biblical quotations wherever she could find them. However, in her early youth the book that nourished her spiritual life was the *Imitation of Christ* by the medieval monk

Thomas à Kempis. She knew it by heart and it remained for her a point of reference up to the end of her life. Later, at the ages of seventeen and eighteen years, she said that she found much illumination in the works of St. John of the Cross, but then she discovered Holy Scripture, particularly the Gospel, and this became the main source of her spiritual nourishment. She wrote in her autobiography:

> After that, I found that all spiritual books left me as dry as ever, and I'm still like that. I've only to open one – even the finest, even the most affecting of them – to find my heart shut up tight against it; I can't think about what I'm reading, or else it just gets as far as my brain without helping me to meditate at all. I can only escape from this difficulty of mine by reading Holy Scripture and the *Imitation of Christ*; there you have solid, wholemeal nourishment. But above all it's the Gospels that occupy my mind when I'm at prayer; my soul has so many needs, and yet this is the one thing needful. I'm always finding fresh lights there; hidden meanings which had meant nothing to me hitherto.

It is interesting to notice that, without knowing it, Thérèse here uses the same words of the medieval Carthusian monk Guigo, who describing meditation – the second step of the *Lectio Divina* method of praying with the Bible – says that the purpose of meditation is 'to bring out the truth hidden in the text' (the traditional stages of *Lectio Divina* are discussed later in this book by Joseph Chalmers). Thérèse returns to this same image in one of her poems in which she says to Jesus: 'Show me the secrets hidden in the Gospel. Ah! This golden book is my most cherished treasure!' In a letter to Céline she wrote: 'Again and again we come down into the fertile valleys where our hearts love to pasture; the vast field of Scripture, which had so often opened before us to spread its rich treasures for our profit.' We believe that we have here an allusion to the parable of Jesus on the treasure hidden in a field. Quite often, speaking of her reading of Holy Scripture, Thérèse speaks of 'searching' and 'finding'.

Holy Scripture illuminates the spiritual journey for Thérèse and others

But what was it that Thérèse searched for in the Bible? She searched for illumination for her spiritual journey and for that of others. She sought to understand what she and others were going through in the light of the word of God. The Bible provided her with an answer to her spiritual problems and confirmed her spiritual intuitions. It was for her like an oracle which she consulted regularly: 'One day, as I was thinking what I could do to save souls, I received light through a word of the Gospel'. Elsewhere she stated: 'After reading your letter, I went to pray, and taking up the Gospels, I begged Jesus that I would find a passage suitable for your situation and this is what I have found ...'

It was the word of God that led Thérèse on from one step to another on her spiritual journey. At the age of fourteen she began to feel the call to work for the salvation of sinners. 'That cry of Our Lord's on the cross – "I am thirsty" – went on echoing in my heart; and they kindled in me a zeal which I'd never known before – how could I allay his thirst for souls, except by sharing it?'

During her pilgrimage to Rome to ask the Pope's permission to enter Carmel at the early age of fifteen, during the Mass which preceded the papal audience, Thérèse says that she:

> ... had a great feeling of confidence; there were those splendid words in the Gospel for the day: "Do not be afraid, you, my little flock. Your Father has determined to give you his kingdom"; and could I doubt that in a short time the kingdom of Carmel would be mine? I had forgotten those other words of Our Lord's about allotting a kingdom to his disciples just as his Father had allotted a kingdom to him: that meant, surely, that they could only prove themselves worthy of their ambition by enduring crosses and trials. It was expected (he told them) that Christ should undergo sufferings, and enter so into his glory; no sitting at his side until they had drunk of his own cup. Well, I was to drink the cup the Holy Father gave me, a cup of bitterness, not without tears.

But it was especially in Thérèse's discovery of the 'Little Way' and of her vocation in the Church that Holy Scripture played a fundamental role.

The Bible and Thérèse's 'Little Way of Spiritual Childhood'

Towards the end of 1894 or the beginning of 1895, Thérèse was devoured with the desire to become a great saint, but at the same time she felt the whole weight of her imperfections. So she began to look for 'an elevator lift which will take me up to Jesus':

I looked in the Bible for some hint about the elevator lift I wanted, and I came across the passage where Eternal Wisdom says: "Is anyone simple as a little child? Then let him come to me." To that Wisdom I went; it seemed as if I was on the right track; what did God undertake to do for the childlike soul that responded to his invitation? I read on, and this is what I found: "I will console you like a mother caressing her son; you shall be like children carried at the breast, fondled on a mother's lap." Never were words so touching; never was such a music to rejoice the heart – I could, after all, be lifted up to heaven, in the arms of Jesus! And if that was to happen, there was no need for me to grow bigger; on the contrary, I must be as small as ever, smaller than ever!

Around two years after this, Thérèse was enkindled with intense desires; she felt called to be a warrior, a priest, an apostle, a doctor of the Church, a martyr. Again she turned to Holy Scripture for a solution:

I was still being tormented by this question of unfulfilled longings and it was a real martyrdom in my prayer, when I decided to consult St. Paul's epistles in the hopes of getting an answer. It was the twelfth and thirteenth chapters of First Corinthians that claimed my attention. The first of these told me that we can't all of us be apostles, all of us be prophets, all of us doctors, and so on; the Church is composed of members which differ in their use; the eye is one thing and the hand is another. It was a clear enough answer, but it didn't satisfy my aspirations, didn't set my heart at rest. The Magdalen, by stooping now and again into the empty tomb, was at last rewarded for her search; and I, sinking down into the depths of my own nothingness, rose high enough to find what I wanted! Reading on to the end of the chapter, I met this comforting phrase: 'Prize the best gifts of heaven. Meanwhile, I can show you a way which is better than any other.' What was that? The Apostle goes on to explain that all the gifts of heaven, even the most perfect of them, without love, are absolutely nothing; charity is the best way of all, because it leads straight to God. Now I was at peace; when St. Paul was talking about the different members of the Mystical Body I couldn't recognise myself in any of them; or rather I could recognise myself in all of them. But charity – that was the key to my vocation. If the Church was a body composed of different members, it couldn't lack the noblest of all; it must have a heart, a heart burning with love.

And I realised that this love was the true motive force which enabled the other members of the Church to act; that if it ceased to function the Apostles would forget to preach the gospel, the martyrs would refuse to shed their blood. Love, in fact, is the vocation which contains all other vocations, love is everything. It knows no limit of time or space for it is eternal. Then, bursting with delirious joy, I exclaimed: 'Oh Jesus, my Love, I have found my vocation at last, my vocation is love! Yes, I have found my place in the Church and this place was given to me by you, oh my God! In the heart of the Church my mother, I shall be love. This way I shall be everything ... and my dream will be fulfilled!

Yet there were times when this living source from which Thérèse drank so abundantly dried up. The oracle remained without word. In one of her letters, Thérèse shared with her sister Céline: "... that vast field [of Scripture] seems like an arid and waterless desert; we no longer even know where we are: instead of peace, light, we find only trouble or at least darkness ..."

Holy Scripture is Jesus

It is not only for illumination or clarification that Thérèse looked in the Bible. Above all, she looked for and discovered in it the word of her Beloved. In the first manuscript of her autobiography, Thérèse said that in the Gospel accounts she finds all that she needs for her spiritual life, before adding:

It's an experience that makes me understand what's meant by the text, "The Kingdom of God is here, within you." Our Lord doesn't need to make use of books or teachers in the instruction of souls; isn't he himself the Teacher of all teachers, conveying knowledge with never a word spoken? For myself, I have never heard the sound of his voice, but I know that he dwells within all the time, guiding me and inspiring me whenever I do or say anything.

That's why Thérèse loved Holy Scripture so much: through it she met Jesus speaking to her. It was the same experience of Saint Bernard who wrote: 'The thirsty soul loves to prolong her contact with Holy Scripture because she knows that there she will find the One she thirsts for.' Speaking of Saint Cecilia, Thérèse wrote: 'Her life was nothing but a melodious song even in the midst of harsh trials and this doesn't marvel me since "she used to keep the holy gospel close to her heart" and in her heart dwelt the Bridegroom of the virgins.' Thus Thérèse intuitively understood that 'the whole Bible constitutes a single book and that book is Christ', as the learned medieval monk Hugh of Saint-Victor had written. In a letter to Céline, Thérèse wrote: 'To keep Jesus's word – that is the sole condition of our happiness, the proof of our love for him. But what is this word? … It seems to me that Jesus' word is Himself, Jesus, the Word, the Word of God!'

God's words became Thérèse's words

It is clear therefore that Thérèse approached Holy Scripture convinced that when she read the Bible she was in fact listening to Jesus who was speaking to her through the sacred books. But there is still another aspect in her use of the Bible that we would like to mention. Thérèse prayed with the Bible not only in the sense of listening prayerfully to the Word of God contained in the Scriptures, but also in the sense that she used the very words of Scripture to express her feelings to God:

> Entering my cell, I began to wonder what Jesus was thinking. Immediately I recalled the words He addressed one day to the adulterous woman: "Does anyone condemn you?" And with tears in my eyes I answered Him: "No one, Lord … neither my little Mother, the image of Your love, nor Sister, the image of Your justice; and I feel that I may surely go in peace, for you do not condemn me either."

But perhaps the most beautiful example of Thérèse's use of the Bible to formulate her own personal prayer is found in the last pages of Manuscript C of her autobiography, where she writes a beautiful prayer using the words of Jesus himself in Chapter 17 of the Gospel of John.

Conclusion

One of the characteristics of St. Thérèse of Lisieux is that both in her experience and in her doctrine she insists on what is really important in the Christian message and in the spiritual life. This is true also with regard to Holy Scripture. Thérèse is one of the most eloquent examples of how important the Word of God should be in our life. With her we learn to read our daily experience in the light of the Word of God, to encounter Jesus in his Word and to speak to the Father using the same words He addresses to us.

This article was printed in the international periodical for Lay Carmelites, *Carmel in the World*, Volume XXXVII, Numbers 1-2, (Rome: Edizioni Carmelitane, 1988), pp. 73-82.

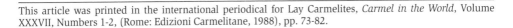

Remember that as a child of light

I often forget to serve my King well.

Oh! Take pity on my great misery.

In your love, Jesus, forgive me.

Make me wise in the ways of Heaven.

Show me the secrets hidden in the Gospel.

Ah! that golden book

Is my dearest treasure,

Remember.

Saint Thérèse of Lisieux, 'Jesus, My Beloved, Remember', translated by Donald Kinney, O.C.D., in The Poetry of Saint Thérèse of Lisieux, *p. 126.*

Thérèse, the Carmelite way of life, and the Bible

Johan Bergström-Allen, T.O.C., & Hugh Clarke, O.Carm.

As a young girl in nineteenth-century France, Thérèse Martin was influenced by a number of people, things, ideas and events: the death of her mother whilst Thérèse was just a child; the *Imitation of Christ* by Thomas à Kempis; the entry of her sisters into a Carmelite monastery of nuns; her father's tender care for her, and his later psychological breakdown; a pilgrimage to Rome; political events in the world, and so on.

The Bible: a guide for life and a mirror of life

One of the most important and life-transforming influences on Thérèse Martin was her contact with God's Word in the Bible, the Holy Scriptures. In reading and meditating upon the Bible, Thérèse was given a vision of God's kingdom which deeply appealed to her. She recognised the Bible not simply as a set of rules or a compendium of historical myths but rather as a collection of stories about God's love for Creation, especially for humanity. Most importantly, she encountered in the Gospels – the accounts of Jesus of Nazareth – the real and living presence of the Son of God.

In the opening chapter of Manuscript A of her autobiography, *Story of a Soul*, Thérèse describes the process of writing her life story, which involved prayer and 'opening the Holy Gospels' for inspiration. In opening the accounts of Christ's life, Thérèse found within echoes of her own life and religious vocation.

Today all Christians of every denomination are encouraged to read the Bible regularly, but in France in the 1800s there was some suspicion of doing so. Since the time of the Reformation, the Roman Catholic Church had been nervous about encouraging 'ordinary people' to take up the Bible, which was read out in Church in Latin, or depicted in art, but not generally available in people's homes. Some clergy were nervous that untrained and barely literate lay people might misunderstand the Scriptures, or read them out of context without clerical supervision. Protestant reformers had broken away from the Roman Catholic Church over this and related issues, and reading the Bible was sometimes perceived as an indication of heresy. Book production was expensive, and it was often only the rich who could afford to have a copy in their homes.[1]

---

1 On the forms of Scripture available to lay people and nuns in nineteenth-century France, see John Russell, O.Carm., 'Saint Thérèse of Lisieux and Scripture', in Keith J. Egan & Craig E. Morrison, (eds.), *Master of the Sacred Page: Essays and Articles in Honor of Roland E. Murphy, O.Carm.*, (Washington D.C.: The Carmelite Institute, 1997) pp. 335-51.

The Bible in the Churches today

Thanks be to God this attitude of suspicion towards Bible reading has changed drastically in the last century, particularly since the Second Vatican Council in the 1960s. The Roman Catholic Church has rediscovered its love of the Scriptures, allowing for a new outpouring of the Holy Spirit, as well as a coming together of different Christian traditions. Pope Benedict XVI has encouraged Catholics and others to read the Bible with new vigour, not only studying it but also engaging in the prayerful meditation on Scripture known as *Lectio Divina* (a guide to which you'll find in Joseph Chalmers' chapter in this book). Initiatives such as the 'Year of Saint Paul' and the Synod of Bishops in Rome on 'The Word of God in the Church' (both in 2008) have also highlighted the central place of the Bible in Catholic Christian communities.

Of course Thérèse lived before the Second Vatican Council. How did she come to know and to love the Bible as the revelation of God's Word?

Carmelite love for God's Word

Part of the answer to the question of how Thérèse came to know and love the Bible can be found in the fact that Thérèse became a Carmelite nun at the age of fifteen. Although it is unlikely that the monastery she entered in Lisieux had a complete copy of the Bible (on this see the preceding chapter by Alexander Vella), the Carmelite tradition of prayer and spirituality placed great importance upon the Word of God. To appreciate the love Thérèse had for God's Word, it's helpful to know something about the close bond between the Carmelites and the Bible.[2]

What is now the international Carmelite Order began around the year 1200 as a small community of hermits gathered on the mountain range known as Mount Carmel in the Holy Land. Carmel had been revered as a holy place since the time of the Old Testament prophet Elijah (possibly even earlier), and sometime around the start of the thirteenth century a group of Christian hermits assembled together in a community to live the contemplative life,

---

2   This article is intended to give only a brief overview of Thérèse's love of Scripture in the context of the Carmelite way of life. For a more detailed and excellent consideration of the link between Carmel and the Word of See, see James McCaffrey, O.C.D., *The Carmelite Charism: Exploring the Biblical Roots*, (Dublin: Veritas, 2004), and by the same author *Captive Flames: A Biblical Reading of the Carmelite Saints*, (Dublin: Veritas, 2005). Other masterful discussions by Carmelites of the link between their Order and the Bible include: Carlos Mesters, O.Carm., *Defenceless Flower: A New Reading of the Bible*, (London: CIIR, 1989); Keith J. Egan, T.O.C., & Craig E. Morrison, O.Carm., (eds.), *Master of the Sacred Page: Essays and Articles in Honor of Roland E. Murphy, O.Carm.*, (Washington D.C.: The Carmelite Institute, 1997); Carlos Mesters, O.Carm., 'Lectio Divina' in *Horizons*, Carmelite Spiritual Directory Project volume 10, (Melbourne: Carmelite Communications, 1999); Joseph Chalmers, O.Carm., 'Hearing the Word', in *Mary the Contemplative*, (Rome: Edizioni Carmelitane, 2001), pp. 35-52; Roland E. Murphy, *Experiencing Our Biblical Heritage*, (Peabody, Massachusetts: Hendrickson, 2001).

blending prayer with service of each other and of the pilgrims who came to the mountain en route to the holy places.

The Carmelite *Rule of Saint Albert*

Those hermits eventually approached the Latin Patriarch (Roman Catholic Bishop) of Jerusalem, Saint Albert Avogadro, to ask him to approve a document setting out their way of life. This text, which eventually became known as *The Rule of Saint Albert*, stipulated that the prayerful reading of the Bible was to be given a central role in Carmelite existence. Of course all Christians are now encouraged to take up the Bible regularly, but in the Middle Ages contact with the 'Sacred Page' (as the Bible was known) was not always widespread and was often second-hand. There is no one single 'method' of Carmelite prayer, but the *Rule of Saint Albert* makes it clear that attentiveness to hearing God in silence and in the Scriptures is a strong component in the Carmelite tradition.[3]

The *Rule of Saint Albert* which Thérèse followed as a Carmelite nun was focussed entirely on Jesus Christ. In approving a document setting out the way that Carmelites should live, the Patriarch of Jerusalem echoed the words of Saint Paul: 'live a life of allegiance to Jesus Christ, and pure in heart and stout in conscience, be unswerving in the service of the Master'. This is just one of many references and allusions to Scripture that Saint Albert included in the Carmelite *Rule*.

The law of the Lord

The way of life document which Saint Albert gave to the hermits is not a long *Rule* by the standards of contemporary medieval religious orders – just 24 short paragraphs or chapters (the whole *Rule* is printed at the end of this article). Within those 24 chapters, many consider Chapter 10 to be at its very heart:

> All the brothers are to remain in their cells or near them, meditating day and night on the law of the Lord, and being vigilant in prayers, unless otherwise lawfully occupied.

---

3 A good recent introduction to the *Rule of Saint Albert* is Patrick Thomas McMahon, *A Pattern for Life: The Rule of Saint Albert and the Carmelite Laity*, Carmel in the World Paperbacks 14, (Rome: Edizioni Carmelitane, 2007). A scholarly study of the link between Saint Albert, his *Rule*, and Scripture is given by the Carmelite Bible scholar Craig Morrison, O.Carm., in Evaldo Xavier Gomes, Patrick McMahon, Simon Nolan, Vincenzo Mosca (eds.), *The Carmelite Rule 1207-2007: Proceedings of the Lisieux Conference 4-7 July 2005*, Institutum Carmelitanum Textus et Studia Historica Carmelitana 28, (Rome: Edizioni Carmelitane, 2008).

The term 'law of the Lord' has been interpreted by Carmelites as meaning both the person of Jesus Christ (who came as the fulfilment of God's law), and the Bible, the Word of God. Meditating on God and God's teachings is therefore central to the Carmelite project which Saint Thérèse engaged in. The *Rule of Saint Albert* is characterised by a very strong devotion to the Word of God in both Scripture and in the person of Jesus Christ. The *Rule* encouraged the hermits to 'live in allegiance to Jesus Christ', serving him unswervingly (Chapter 2). This focus on Jesus in the *Rule* of the Carmelite Order was to make a great impact on Thérèse's close relationship with him. Thérèse of Lisieux was truly Carmelite in her love of the Word of God, both in the person of Jesus Christ, and in the Bible. As Fr. Vella said in the preceding article, 'Thérèse approached Holy Scripture convinced that when she read the Bible she was in fact listening to Jesus who was speaking to her through the sacred books'.

We cannot stress sufficiently: Christ is the Alpha and Omega of the Carmelite *Rule*. The *Rule* begins and ends in Jesus Christ. To live in the service of Christ and to live devotedly in Christ: in these words of Saint Paul the first Carmelites outlined to Saint Albert (who approved their document) the fundamental purpose of their hermit way of life. They were simply to serve Christ by nurturing a close relationship with Christ. They were to imitate Christ in his prayer at night on the mountain and to keep watch with him in the garden.

The Bible and prayer

The central precept of the *Rule of Saint Albert* concerns the Bible and prayer, the basic activity of the Carmelite: 'Each one of you is to stay in his (or her) cell or nearby, pondering the law of the Lord day and night and keeping watch at prayers unless attending to some other duty' (Chapter 10). In its simplicity this reminds us of the words of the other great medieval Lawgiver, Saint Benedict, who simply states in his *Rule* that 'If a monk is so inclined, let him go into the chapel and pray'. No further directives are given as regards prayer in either the Carmelite or the Benedictine *Rules*. Prayer must always involve a fundamental attitude to God, the attitude of wanting nothing but the will of the Father. This must underlie any view of prayer, as it did that of Jesus himself who always did the things which pleased his heavenly Father. 'To live a life of allegiance to Jesus Christ', to love Jesus, involves a relationship which must begin and end in prayer, for, as Jesus himself is the Son of God and is in continual communion with his Father, so also must be the one who has promised to follow him.

Prayer is simplicity itself, once this fundamental relationship – this friendship between God the Father and his children – is appreciated. Thérèse knew herself to be a little child of God, that God was her 'Papa', her 'Daddy' (and also 'more tender than a mother'). Thérèse wanted to talk to God, to be with God as much as possible. In the *Rule of Saint Albert* silence is enjoined as a means of being open to God. On one occasion when asked what she said to God, Thérèse replied 'I don't say anything to him; I love him.' Silence in the loving presence of God is the highest form of prayer, and is in the true line of Carmelite spirituality which seeks to help us be contemplatives, that is, friends with God who are open to the inpouring of the Spirit.

Encountering the Word in many places

Even before Thérèse entered Carmel it was Jesus who ravished her heart. Once inside the monastery Thérèse's love was nourished and nurtured by the focus on Jesus found in the *Rule of Saint Albert*. The *Rule* formed part of the book containing the *Constitutions* of the Discalced Carmelite Order which Thérèse was expected to read and study.

Thérèse would therefore have known that the *Rule of Saint Albert* had more to say about the Bible, such as Chapter 7, which states that the Carmelites should 'eat in a common refectory ... listening together to a reading from Holy Scripture'. Thérèse would have heard Bible passages regularly not only in the refectory dining-room at the Carmel in Lisieux, but also when the community attended the celebration of the Eucharist and the Divine Office, liturgies that presented passages of Scripture to ruminate on. Such communal prayer is also specified in the Carmelite *Rule*: 'Those who know their letters [how to read] and how to read the psalms should for each of the canonical hours say those our holy forefathers laid down and the approved custom of the Church appoints for that hour' (Chapter 11). Praying the Psalter – the Book of Psalms – is a characteristic form of prayer for the Carmelite.

The Psalms and the Divine Office

What place did the psalms and the Office play in the life of Saint Thérèse? We know indeed what joy she found in those words inspired by the Holy Spirit. Those who know both the psalms and the writings of Thérèse will appreciate how often the sentiments of the psalms and often the very words inspire her own writings (as we can see in a later section of this book). The Psalter is the book of the Old Testament most quoted by Thérèse. In the psalms Thérèse found an echo of her own thoughts and desires. A child of God, always looking towards God as to her Father and Mother, whose arms she never left, Thérèse found instinctively in the psalms the expressions which could translate her own feelings. Just as those psalms were constantly on the lips of Christ himself, so also were they the daily expression of the attitude of Thérèse to her heavenly Father.

The teaching and example of Saint Paul

The second half of the *Rule of Saint Albert* consists largely of quotations from Scripture, especially the writings of Saint Paul who was very influential in the life of Saint Thérèse. In Chapter 19 of the *Rule* Saint Albert states:

> The sword of the Spirit, which is the word of God, is to dwell abundantly in your mouths and hearts. So whatever you have to do is to be done in the word of the Lord.

These are words Thérèse took to heart, as she did the advice contained in Chapter 20:

> You have both the teaching and the example of Blessed Paul the Apostle; Christ spoke through his mouth; he has been set up and given by God as a preacher and teacher of the nations in faith and truth; in following him you cannot go wrong.

The love of Holy Scripture is therefore part of the very fabric of the Carmelite way of life; as the Carmelite Bible scholar Carlos Mesters says, a vibrant engagement with the Bible is part of the Carmelite Order's DNA.[4] Since the *Rule of Saint Albert* was given to the hermits on Mount Carmel centuries ago, their descendents – the hermits, friars, enclosed nuns, active sisters, and lay members of the Carmelite Family – have nourished their relationships with God particularly through meditation of God's living Word.

Thérèse: the Doctor of Love taught by God's Word

In 1997 Pope John Paul II declared Saint Thérèse a Doctor of the Universal Church, that is, a pre-eminent teacher of Christian doctrine, and she has been nicknamed the *Doctor Amoris* ('Doctor of Love'). In his apostolic letter marking

---

4   For a guide to *Lectio Divina* by Carlos Mesters, O.Carm., see John FitzGerald, *Backwards into the Future: Meditations on the Letter to the Hebrews*, (Faversham: Saint Albert's Press, 2005), pp. 127-37, also available online at the website of the British Province of Carmelites: www.carmelite.org.

the occasion, *Divini Amoris Scientia*, the Pope frequently pointed out how Thérèse's writings, including her poetry, were inspired by the reading of the Word of God:

§7 This young Carmelite, without any particular theological training, but illumined by the light of the Gospel, feels she is being taught by the divine Teacher who, as she says, is "the Doctor of Doctors" (Ms. A, 83v), and from him she receives "divine teachings" (Ms. B, 1r). She feels that the words of Scripture are fulfilled in her: "Whoever is a little one, let him come to me ... For to him that is little, mercy shall be shown" (Ms. B, 1v; cf. *Proverbs* 9:4; *Wisdom* 6:6) and she knows she is being instructed in the science of love, hidden from the wise and prudent, which the divine Teacher deigned to reveal to her, as to babes (Ms. A, 49r; cf. *Luke* 10:21-22).

§9 The primary source of her spiritual experience and her teaching is the Word of God in the Old and New Testaments. She herself admits it, particularly stressing her passionate love for the Gospel (cf. Ms. A, 83v). Her writings contain over 1,000 biblical quotations: more than 400 from the Old Testament and over 600 from the New. Despite her inadequate training and lack of resources for studying and interpreting the sacred books, Thérèse immersed herself in meditation on the Word of God with exceptional faith and spontaneity. Under the influence of the Holy Spirit she attained a profound knowledge of Revelation for herself and for others. By her loving concentration on Scripture – she even wanted to learn Hebrew and Greek to understand better the spirit and letter of the sacred books – she showed the importance of the biblical sources in the spiritual life, she emphasized the originality and freshness of the Gospel, she cultivated with moderation the spiritual exegesis of the Word of God in both the Old and New Testaments. Thus she discovered hidden treasures, appropriating words and episodes, sometimes with supernatural boldness, as when, in reading the texts of Saint Paul (cf. *1 Corinthians* 12-13), she realized her vocation to love (cf. Ms. B, 3r-3v). Enlightened by the revealed Word, Thérèse wrote brilliant pages on the unity between love of God and love of neighbour (cf. Ms. C, 11v-19r); and she identified with Jesus's prayer at the Last Supper as the expression of her intercession for the salvation of all (cf. Ms. C, 34r-35r).

The apostolic letter *Divini Amoris Scientia* praises Thérèse's grasp of the mysterious love of God that she gained through attentively listening to and reading of the Scriptures.

God's Word is a light in the dark

Towards the end of her short life on earth, Thérèse experienced the 'dark night' that fellow Carmelite Saint John of the Cross wrote of as a normal part of the spiritual journey, in which she could not feel the presence of God, relying solely on faith. The writings of John of the Cross helped her for a time, but eventually only the Scriptures were enough to guide her in the darkness:

> Ah! how many lights have I not drawn from the works of our holy Father, St. John of the Cross! At the ages of seventeen and eighteen I had no other spiritual nourishment; later on, however, all books left me in aridity and I'm still in that state. If I open a book composed by a spiritual author (even the most beautiful, the most touching book), I feel my heart contract immediately and I read without understanding, so to speak. Or if I do understand, my mind comes to a standstill without the capacity of meditating. In this helplessness, Holy Scripture and the *Imitation* [*of Christ* by Thomas à Kempis] come to my aid; in them I discover a solid and very *pure* nourishment. But it is especially the *Gospels* which sustain me during my hours of prayer, for in them I find what is necessary for my poor little soul. I am constantly discovering in them new lights, hidden and mysterious meanings.
>
> I understand and I know from experience that: *The kingdom of God is within you.* Jesus has no need of books or teachers to instruct souls; He teaches without the noise of words. Never have I heard Him speak, but I feel that He is within me at each moment; He is guiding and inspiring me with what I must say and do. I find just when I need them certain lights which I had not seen until then, and it isn't most frequently during my hours of prayer that these are most abundant but rather in the midst of my daily occupations.
>
> O my dear Mother! after so many graces can I not sing with the Psalmist: *How GOOD is the Lord, his MERCY endures forever!*[5]

---

5   *Story of a Soul*, Manuscript A, Chapter VIII, trans. John Clarke, pp. 179-80.

This passage makes it clear that during the eighteen-month period of doubt and darkness that engulfed her, Thérèse found light in the Gospels. Her emptiness was filled by God's own self, allowing her to echo the words of the Psalmist that God is good and merciful.[6]

Discovering new lights

Thérèse learned to turn to the Sacred Page whenever she sought confirmation of an idea. She also had no difficulty in seeing the relevance of the Bible for her own times, invoking a very contemporary image:

> We are living now in an age of inventions, and we no longer have to take the trouble of climbing stairs, for, in the homes of the rich, an elevator has replaced these very successfully. I wanted to find an elevator which would raise me to Jesus, for I am too small to climb the rough stairway of perfection. I searched, then, in the Scriptures for some sign of this elevator, the object of my desires, and I read these words coming from the mouth of Eternal Wisdom: *Whoever is a LITTLE ONE, let him come to me.* And so I succeeded. I felt I had found what I was looking for. But wanting to know, O my God, what You would do to *the very little one* who answered Your call, I continued my search and this is what I discovered: *As one whom a mother caresses, so will I comfort you; you shall be carried at the breasts and upon the knees they shall caress you.* Ah! never did words more tender and more melodious come to give joy to my soul. The elevator which must raise me to heaven is Your arms, O Jesus! And for this I had no need to grow up, but rather I had to remain *little* and become this more and more.[7]

In this exquisite passage Thérèse quotes from two books of the Old Testament (*Proverbs* 9:4 and *Isaiah* 66:13, 12), discovering in them the maternal love of God which will carry her to Christ. The 'littleness' of which she speaks is her famous 'Little Way' of childlike confidence and trust in God. Though revolutionary in many respects, Thérèse's 'doctrine' was rooted in her reading of the Old Testament. In that sense it was truly 'radical', returning to the roots.

---

6   On Thérèse's Gospel-rooted trust in God's mercy and grace, see John Welch, O.Carm., 'Saint Thérèse's Discovery of Merciful Love', in Keith J. Egan & Craig E. Morrison, (eds.), *Master of the Sacred Page: Essays and Articles in Honor of Roland E. Murphy, O.Carm.*, (Washington D.C.: The Carmelite Institute, 1997) pp. 389-401.
7   *Story of a Soul*, Manuscript C, trans. John Clarke, pp. 207-08.

The Little Way: an echo of the Good News

'Whoever makes themselves small like a little child shall be great in the kingdom of heaven'.
Sculpture on the façade of the Basilica of Saint Thérèse in Lisieux.

The 'Little Way' for which Thérèse is rightly renowned is essentially a re-stating of the Bible narratives of God's love for his people. The Little Way is an echo of the Gospel – the Good News that God loves us and desires to be our closest friend. Thérèse saw that in the Gospel 'The law of fear has been replaced by the law of love'. In speaking thus Thérèse was thinking of the New Testament as compared with the Old Testament, but in fact we can apply the same words to the revolution which she introduced into our whole concept of God and God's relationship with us, something which is rooted in Scripture but which it took a 'Little Flower' like Thérèse to remind the Church of.

The Bible: a record of God's passionate desire for us

We know that Thérèse wanted to compose a commentary on *The Song of Songs* and what a pity it is that she was never able to do so. Some time ago a former archbishop was asked what he would do if he had to edit the Bible; he replied that he would try to make it a better guide to behaviour and to morals. For this reason he would leave out certain passages, including the whole of *The Song of Songs*. He felt it was not a suitable guide to moral behaviour, since it describes in intimate terms the love of bride and bridegroom. With all due respect to an archbishop, that attitude is completely wrong, since the Bible was never intended to be a book of etiquette. Primarily it is intended to reveal our relationship with God and God's love for us. In this context *The Song of Songs* finds a natural place – and a fond place in the hearts of many Carmelites – since our relationship is in the nature of a love affair.[8] It is in understanding this that the genius of Thérèse lies, under the guidance of the Holy Spirit.

---

8   John Welch, O.Carm., makes the observation that 'the Carmelite tradition could be understood as an 800 year commentary on *The Song of Songs*' in his talk at the 2001 General Chapter of the Carmelite Order, entitled *Seasons of the Heart: The Spiritual Dynamic of the Carmelite Life*. This talk has been published in various formats and is also available on the website of the British Province of Carmelites: www.carmelite.org.

Openness to God

From *The Song of Songs*, the gospel accounts, and other passages of Scripture, Thérèse learnt how to open herself to God. As James McCaffrey puts it later in this book, 'Thérèse is in touch with her own infinite emptiness for God'. Thérèse practiced a spirit and attitude of the heart that the Carmelite tradition refers to as *Vacare Deo*, literally 'openness to God', or 'making space for God'. In letting herself be infused with God's Word, Thérèse showed the same spirit of *Vacare Deo* that allowed the Blessed Virgin Mary to speak using the very words of Scripture (namely *Isaiah* 61) during her *Magnificat* (*Luke* 1:46-55). In her openness to God and ability to speak in the words of Scripture Thérèse was also a true daughter of Saint Albert of Jerusalem, who (as discussed in the next chapter of this book) echoed numerous Bible passages when writing the Carmelite *Rule* that Thérèse followed.

Conclusion

Thérèse of Lisieux was rooted in the Carmelite tradition which encouraged her voracious appetite for the Word of God, and which in turn fuelled and expressed her passion for Jesus Christ. Thérèse's wisdom is a new articulation of the ancient wisdom of Carmel, gifts of God for the benefit of the Church and humanity. It is surely no accident that the declaration of Thérèse as a Doctor of the Church has coincided with a renewed interest in the study of Scripture and a revived commitment to the prayerful pondering of God's Word. Thérèse is an inspiration for all Christians to encounter God's Word on a daily basis and to share it with others by the way that we live 'in allegiance to Jesus Christ'.

Thérèse found that in the 'Garden of Carmel', the soil must be fertilised by the Word of God. As God said through the prophet Isaiah (55:10-12):

> For as the rain and the snow come down from heaven,
>   and do not return there until they have watered the earth,
> making it bring forth and sprout,
>   giving seed to the sower and bread to the eater,
> so shall my word be that goes out from my mouth;
>   it shall not return to me empty,
> but it shall accomplish that which I purpose,
>   and succeed in the thing for which I sent it.

Some of the material in this chapter is adapted from the late Hugh Clarke's *Message of Love: Reflections on the Life of St. Thérèse*, (Faversham: The Carmelite Press, 1976), pp. 50-55.

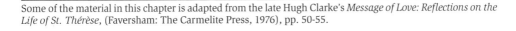

Thérèse depicted in stained glass at Gibraltar Catholic Cathedral.

The Rule of Saint Albert

translated by Christopher O'Donnell, O.Carm.

As a Carmelite nun, Saint Thérèse would have known and reflected on the vision of her Order as set out in *The Rule of Saint Albert*, which places great emphasis upon the importance of Scripture (as discussed in the previous chapter). The numbers in brackets refer to the older chapter numbering previously used by different branches of the Carmelite Family.

1   [Prologue, i] Albert, called by the grace of God to be Patriarch of the Church of Jerusalem, greets his beloved sons in Christ, B. and the other hermits living in obedience to him near the spring on Mount Carmel: salvation in the Lord and the blessing of the Holy Spirit.

2   [Prologue, ii] Many times and in different ways the holy Fathers have laid down that everyone – whatever be their state in life or the religious life chosen by them – should live under the patronage of Jesus Christ and serve him zealously with a pure heart and a good conscience.

3   Now then you have come to me seeking a formula of life according to your proposed manner of life, which you are to observe in the future.

4   [I, iii] The first thing I lay down is that you shall have a prior, one of yourselves, chosen by the unanimous consent of all, or of the greater and more mature part. All the others shall promise him obedience fulfilling it by deeds, as well as chastity and the renunciation of property.

5   [II, iv] You can take up places in solitary areas or in sites given to you, one suitable and convenient for your observance in the judgment of the prior and the brothers.

6   [III, v] Moreover, taking account of the site you propose to occupy, all of you are to have separate cells; these are to be assigned by the prior himself with the agreement of the other brothers or the more mature of them.

7   [IV, vi] You are, however, to eat in a common refectory what may have been given to you, listening together to a reading from holy Scripture, if this can conveniently be done.

8 [V, vii] No brother is permitted to change the place assigned to him or exchange with another, unless with the permission of the prior at the time.

9 [VI] The prior's cell shall be near the entrance to the place so that he may first meet those who come to the place and everything afterwards may be done as he decides and arranges.

10 [VII, viii] All are to remain in their cells or near them, meditating day and night on the law of the Lord and being vigilant in prayers, unless otherwise lawfully occupied.

11 [VIII, ix] Those who have learned to say the canonical hours with the clerics should do so according to the practice of the holy Fathers and the approved custom of the Church. Those who do not know the hours are to say the *Our Father* twenty-five times for the night office, except for Sunday and solemn feasts when this number is doubled, so that the *Our Father* is said fifty times. It is to be said seven times for the morning Lauds and for the other Hours, except for Vespers when it must be said fifteen times.

12 [IX, x] None of the brothers is to claim something as his own; everything is to be in common and is to be distributed to each one by the Prior – that is, the brother deputed by him to this office – having regard to the age and needs of each one.

13 [xi] You may have asses or mules according to your needs and some rearing of animals or poultry.

14 [X, xii] An oratory is to be built as conveniently as possible in the midst of the cells; you are to gather daily in the morning for Mass, where this is convenient.

15 [XI, xiii] On Sundays, or other days if necessary, you shall discuss the the preservation of order and the salvation of souls; at this time excesses and faults of the brothers, if such come to light, are to be corrected with boundless charity.

16 [XII, xiv] You are to fast every day except Sundays from the feast of the Exaltation of the Cross until Easter Sunday, unless illness or bodily

weakness, or other just cause counsels a lifting of the fast, since necessity has no law.

17 [XIII, xv] You are to abstain from meat, unless it is to be taken as a remedy for illness or bodily weakness. Since you must more frequently beg on journeys, in order not to burden your hosts you may eat food cooked with meat outside your own houses. At sea, however, meat may be eaten.

18 [XIV, xvi] Since human life on earth is a trial and all who want to live devotedly in Christ suffer persecution; your enemy the devil prowls about like a roaring lion seeking whom he might devour. You must then with all diligence put on the armour of God so that you may be able to stand up to the ambushes of the enemy.

19 Your loins are to be girded with the belt of chastity; your breast is to be protected by holy thoughts, for the Scripture says, holy thoughts will save you. Put on the breastplate of justice, so that you may love the Lord your God from your whole heart, your whole soul and your whole strength, and your neighbour as yourselves. In all things take up the shield of faith, with which you will be able to extinguish all the darts of the evil one; without faith, indeed, it is impossible to please God. The helmet of salvation is to be placed on your head, so that you may hope for salvation from the one Saviour, who saves his people from their sins. The sword of the Spirit, which is the word of God, is to dwell abundantly in your mouths and hearts. So whatever you have to do is to be done in the word of the Lord.

20 [XV, xvii] You should do some work, so that the devil will always find you occupied and he may not through your idleness find some entrance to your souls. In this matter you have both the teaching and the example of Blessed Paul the Apostle; Christ spoke through his mouth; he has been set up and given by God as a preacher and teacher of the nations in faith and truth; in following him you cannot go wrong. In work and weariness, he said, we have been with you, working day and night so as not to be a burden to you; it was not as though we had no right, but we wished to give ourselves as a model for imitation. For when we were with you, we gave this precept: whoever is unwilling to work shall not eat. We have heard that there are restless people going around who do nothing. We condemn such people and implore them in the Lord Jesus Christ that working in silence they should earn their bread. This is a good and holy way: follow it.

Statue of Thérèse in the Basilica of Notre Dame in Geneva, Switzerland.

21 [XVI, xviii] The apostle therefore recommends silence, when he tells us to work in it; the prophet too testifies that silence is the promotion of justice; and again, in silence and in hope will be your strength. Therefore we lay down that from the recitation of Compline you are to maintain silence until after Prime the following day. At other times, though silence is not to be so strictly observed, you are to be diligent in avoiding much talking, since Scripture states and experience likewise teaches, sin is not absent where there is much talking; also he who is careless in speech will experience evil, and the one who uses many words harms his soul. Again the Lord says in the gospel: an account will have to be given on the day of judgement for every vain word. Each of you is to weigh his words and have a proper restraint for his mouth, so that he may not stumble and fall through speech and his fall be irreparable and fatal. He is with the prophet to guard his ways so that he does not offend through the tongue. Silence, which is the promotion of justice, is likewise to be diligently and carefully observed.

22 [XVII, xix] You, Brother B., and whoever is appointed prior after you, shall always keep in mind and practice what the Lord said in the Gospel: Whoever wishes to be greater among you shall be your servant, and whoever wishes to be first must be your slave.

23 [XVIII, xx] And you too, the other brothers are humbly to honour your prior, and rather than thinking about him, you are to look to Christ who set him as head over you; he said to the leaders of the Church, whoever hears you hears me, and whoever despises you despises me. Thus you will not be judged guilty on account of contempt but, on account of obedience you will merit the reward of eternal life.

24 [Epilogue, xxi] I have written these things briefly to you establishing a formula of your common life, according to which you are to conduct yourselves. If anyone does more the Lord himself when he comes again will repay him. You are, however, to use discretion, which is the moderator of virtue.

This translation first appeared in a publication of the Irish Carmelites, *Meeting God: Carmelite Reflections and Prayers*, (Dublin: Columba Press, 2007).

A statue of Thérèse in the Sanctuary of Our Lady of Lourdes, France.

A vocation to love inspired by God's Word

Wilfrid McGreal, O.Carm.

Thérèse Martin, often known as *The Little Flower*, was declared a Doctor of the Church in 1997. This ranks her along with such figures as Augustine, Thomas Aquinas and Teresa of Avila as having some profound insight into the Christian message. Thérèse was not a great writer like Augustine, but she did something crucial: she helped to bring spirituality and theology together again, demonstrating in word and by her life the centrality of prayer and love for theology (the study of the nature of God and religion). She is an important impetus in the Church's rediscovery of the value of the mystical and its moving away from the over-intellectual approach to theology that had been fostered since the seventeenth century.

Thérèse's World and Church

Thérèse had to transcend many aspects of life both in society and in the Church, and even after her death her true self was almost submerged. She was born in Normandy in 1873 into a devout Roman Catholic family, at a time when Roman Catholicism in France was very much on the defensive. Catholics saw themselves as under siege in a rationalist, anti-clerical world. In their retreat to a 'fortress Church', Catholics brought with them an often pietistic faith. There was a retreat into piety and devotion, a withdrawal into a safe space – almost a private world. Allied to a disapproval of secular society and a nostalgia for the ways things were in the *ancien régime,* such Catholics adopted a fierce middle-class respectability; "What will people think?" was often the criterion of behaviour. These attitudes coloured Thérèse's family life and were certainly present in community life in the Carmel (Carmelite monastery of nuns) in Lisieux where she spent the last nine years of her life. It was this spirit of correctness that caused Thérèse's sister to edit her manuscript so that the early editions of *The Story of a Soul* contained radical revisions. Since the 1950s the original manuscripts have been available, and also original photographs that show a more vigorous person, a real human being.

Spirit of creativity

The remarkable aspect of Thérèse's life and ministry was the way she was able to live her years in Carmel with such maturity and creativity. She was the author of her own vision of life and there is a genuine originality in what she wrote and how she lived. Thérèse was a Carmelite in her faithful following of Jesus: he was her guide. Sadly she was not able to immerse herself entirely in the Scriptures after the spirit of the Carmelite *Rule of Saint Albert* because the Bible was not readily available in the French Church of that time (as discussed in previous chapters of this book). Bourgeois susceptibility led to the attitude that many passages of Scripture were too realistic, not 'nice'. The realities of human nature were too much for the post-Jansenist mind. Despite these difficulties, Thérèse was able to read the New Testament and she eventually obtained access to a Bible.

When Teresa of Avila founded her Carmels she wanted them to be communities where friendship could flourish and a simple lifestyle could be realised. She did not want communities to be too large because institutionalism could creep in and financial problems could grow. The Carmel at Lisieux was not entirely in that mould. The community numbered about twenty-five, and it is clear some of the nuns were difficult characters. The prioress, Mother Gonzaga, came from the nobility and never freed herself entirely from her social background. There was tension between her and Thérèse's sisters, and sometimes the community had to wait on the prioress's visiting relatives. The *Rule of Saint Albert* was interpreted with a strictness that missed its essential humanity and was certainly far from Teresa of Avila's creative spirit. Mother Gonzaga was strict in her vision of Carmelite life both for herself and for others. This rage for correctness and the entrenched bourgeois mentality touched Thérèse during her illness when the community went into denial over its nature. For whatever reason, tuberculosis was seen as a disease to be ashamed of – it was an attitude not unlike that adopted today by some people to HIV/AIDS.

Thérèse: true to herself

The great achievement is that Thérèse emerges from this unlikely environment to be so original, creative and self-possessed. She achieved an autonomy that is remarkable, and she was a likeable, strong-minded, humorous and idealistic young woman. She could have been dependent on her sisters, she could have played the games others played, but she found her own place in which to be.

Thérèse always had a lively imagination and a sense of fun. This aspect of her personality enabled her to feel free as a writer, expressive as a poet and fascinated by theatre. She had a great admiration for Joan of Arc, admiring her courage and decisiveness, and there is a striking photograph of her playing the part of the Maid of Orleans in a dramatic presentation she organised for the Carmelite community.

Thérèse acting as Joan of Arc imprisoned, taken in early 1895.

Thérèse's lively imagination links her to the great sixteenth-century Carmelites, Teresa of Avila and John of the Cross. Thérèse shared the great Teresa's romanticism and clear vision. She also lived out in her last months the passive night of the spirit that John of the Cross spoke about in his commentaries. Thérèse knew the writings of the Carmelite Spanish mystics and her teaching on love echoes and repeats John's own words in a new and creative way.[1]

Infusing love into all of life

Thérèse stands at the centre of the Carmelite tradition with her belief that we can all achieve closeness to God through our prayer and our following of Jesus Christ as we live the Gospel. This is her teaching on the 'Little Way'. For Thérèse, holiness, closeness to God, is not achieved by spectacular ascetic practices. We come to God by infusing love into every aspect of life. The 'Little Way' is one of childlike trust in God, but it is not infantile and naïve, or a searching for the lost innocence of some idealised childhood. Thérèse had known through

---

1   See Guy Gaucher, *John and Thérèse: Flames of Love – The Influence of St. John of the Cross in the Life and Writings of St. Thérèse of Lisieux*, (New York: Alba House, 1999).

childhood and early adolescence the pain of separation from those she loved. However, she gained the maturity to realise that trust and consistency were possible, and she began to express them in her wholehearted commitment to God. She wanted a quiet hidden relationship, to live out in secret her love for God. This 'Little Way' was a reaction to the strictness and spectacular ascetic practices that seemed to be demanded by her prioress.

The humanity of Christ

Thérèse was able to come to God in such loving trust because, like Teresa of Avila, she realised that the humanity of Christ was at the heart of Christianity. Jesus is the source of love and happiness for her – the Gospel accounts were her book. However, the most profound insights of Thérèse came during the last eighteen months of her life. Her illness took hold with full seriousness at Easter 1896 and became progressively more painful and crippling. During these last months of her life Thérèse underwent the passive night of the spirit. For her, the experience was one that seemed like the purification of purgatory. She felt she had been placed in darkness and that her belief in God was an illusion. She began to feel that heaven could not exist. It was as if she had been placed in solidarity with non-believers. This struggle was to last until her death. Most difficult of all were the times when she found not just blasphemous thoughts but even blasphemous words welling up inside her. Mocking voices spoke to her, telling her that in the end there was just nothing – it was all an illusion. Thérèse even began to think that science would be able to disprove everything and end up explaining God's existence away. She felt the force of rationalism like a great wave ready to sweep away all traces of belief and, in her own way, she was akin to Matthew Arnold and the grey vision of his poem *Dover Beach*. Even more terrifying for her were suicidal thoughts of ending the pain and the sense of futility:

> Watch carefully, Mother, when you will have patients a prey to violent pains; don't leave them any medicines that are poisonous. I assure you, it needs only a second when one suffers intensely to lose one's reason. Then one would easily poison oneself.

However, just before her death Thérèse was able to say:

> Yes! What a grace it is to have faith. If I had not had faith, I would have committed suicide without an instant's hesitation.[2]

---

2   St. Thérèse of Lisieux, *Her Last Conversations*, trans. John Clarke, (Washington D.C.: I.C.S. Publications, 1977), Aug/258.

Thérèse: a guide on death's journey

In his insightful study on Thérèse, *Love in the Heart of the Church*, Carmelite theologian Chris O'Donnell has shown that Thérèse's experiences have something important to teach us about terminal illness, and may help people face death in an age when there is so much denial about its reality.[3] The doubts and the trial do pass, and in Thérèse's writing we are helped to understand that even in the dark we are not abandoned by God. She is a living commentary on John of the Cross's teaching.

During this time of trial and struggle Thérèse clung on to her relationship with God and tried to express her love in her poems and in her relationships with the community. It was only when she was very near to death that those closest to her became aware of her struggle, and even then perhaps could only guess at what was happening.

Thérèse's clarity of vocation

In the October of 1896 in the middle of her sufferings Thérèse had a moment of light and insight, inspired by the Word of God, which helped her to find a sense of what her life was really about and what her real vocation was. Perhaps it is best to allow her to describe the moment and its import in her own words:

> My desires caused me a veritable martyrdom, and I opened the Epistles of Saint Paul to find some kind of answer. Chapters Twelve and Thirteen of the First Epistle to the Corinthians fell under my eyes. I read there, in the first of these chapters, that *all* cannot be apostles, prophets, doctors, and so on, that the Church is composed of different members, and that the eye cannot be the hand *at one and the same time*. The answer was clear, but it did not fulfil my desires and gave me no peace. Without becoming discouraged, I continued my reading, and this sentence consoled me: '*Yet strive for THE BETTER GIFTS, and I point out to you* a yet more excellent way.' And the Apostle explains how all *the most PERFECT gifts* are nothing without *LOVE*. That *charity is the EXCELLENT WAY* that leads most surely to God.
>
> I finally had to rest. Considering the mystical body of the Church, I had not recognized myself in any of the members described by Saint Paul, or rather I desired to see myself in them *all*. Charity gave me the key to my *vocation*. I understood that if the Church had a body com-

---

3   Christopher O'Donnell, *Love in the heart of the Church - The Mission of Thérèse of Lisieux*, (Dublin: Veritas, 1997).

posed of different members, the most necessary and most noble of all could not be lacking to it, and so I understood that the Church *had a Heart and that this Heart was BURNING WITH LOVE. I understood it was Love alone* that made the Church's members act, that if *Love* ever became extinct, apostles would not preach the Gospel and martyrs would not shed their blood. I understood that LOVE COMPRISED ALL VOCATIONS, THAT LOVE WAS EVERYTHING, THAT IT EMBRACED ALL TIMES AND PLACES ... IN A WORD, THAT IT WAS ETERNAL!

Then, in the excess of my delirious joy, I cried out: 'O Jesus, my Love ... my *vocation*, at last I have found it ... MY VOCATION IS LOVE!'

Yes I have found my place in the Church and it is you, O my God, who have given me this place: in the heart of the Church, my mother, I shall be *Love*. Thus I shall be everything, and thus my dream will be realized.[4]

In communion with God's saints

Thérèse found her vocation in love – love at the heart of the Church. She came to this insight as she read Saint Paul's letters and discovered his teaching on the Mystical Body. This Pauline vision with its emphasis on the Spirit gave Thérèse a generous sense of the Church which helped her to see herself as a missionary even though she never left Carmel. It also enhanced her awareness of the Communion of Saints. This profound awareness of the Church is akin to Teresa of Avila's missionary sense when, in the context of the Reformation, she sought a healing mission in the Church.

One of the rich veins of spirituality that flows from the doctrine of the Communion of Saints is a wonderful appreciation of intercessory prayer. The notion of belonging to a fellowship that goes beyond the here and now is also a powerful antidote to an individualistic approach to salvation.

For Thérèse the saints were her friends. This sense of intimacy began with her attraction to the life of Joan of Arc, but soon extended to other saints and especially to Mary, the Mother of Jesus. She also had a belief that members of her family who had died were part of that community of love and that in a special way a closeness was achieved in the Eucharist between those in heaven and those on earth. Her Church, her community, was one that went beyond the limits of time and space. She spoke to the saints as friends and asked them to intercede for those troubled by doubt or experiencing loss of faith.

---

4   St. Thérèse of Lisieux, *Story of a Soul*, Manuscript B, trans. John Clarke, (Washington D.C.: I.C.S. Publications, 1975), p. 194.

Powerhouse of prayer for missionaries and priests

Thérèse's sense of love being the energy of the Church was the inspiration for her missionary dreams and her support for priests. She had hopes that she might be sent to the Carmel that was being set up in Saigon (now Ho Chi Minh City in Vietnam). However, realising that her health was broken, she turned her energies into a power of love for all involved in that work. She hoped that her prayers, her pain, could support those working to bring the Gospel to remote areas of the world. Once again it was her deep reflection on Paul's teaching that helped her live out the doctrine of the Mystical Body.

Thérèse had a great love for priests and their ministry. It is possible to read her works with our modern eyes and to wonder if she ever wanted to be a priest herself. Certainly her deep sense of communion with Jesus in the Eucharist made her value the liturgy above all else, and she saw the role of those who ministered at the altar as precious. In the last months of her life she was involved in correspondence with two missionary priests. Her enthusiasm and commitment in offering them support and encouragement is amazing given her frail health and the darkness of spirit she was enduring. Her words are full of energy and her warmth of understanding shows her generosity and altruism. She maintained the correspondence almost to the end of her life, and in a poem to Father Roulland, who was ministering in China, she writes:

> Heaven for me is feeling within myself the resemblance
> Of the God who created me with his Powerful Breath.
> Heaven for me is remaining always in his presence,
> Calling him my Father and being his child.
> In his Divine arms, I don't fear the storm.
> Total abandonment is my only law.
> Sleeping on his Heart, right next to his Face,
>   That is Heaven for me! ...

> I've found my Heaven in the Blessed Trinity
> That dwells in my heart, my prisoner of love.
> There, contemplating my God, I fearlessly tell him
> That I want to serve him and love him forever.
> Heaven for me is smiling at this God whom I adore
> When He wants to hide to try my faith.
> To suffer while waiting for him to look at me again
>   That is Heaven for me! ... [5]

5 *The Poetry of St. Thérèse of Lisieux*, trans. Donald Kinney, (Washington D.C.: I.C.S. Publications, 1995), pp. 153-54.

Make love real where you live

Thérèse's greatness is her ability to grasp that the Christian life is the realisation of love in the community where you live. Moreover, that community, if inspired by the dynamic of love, will always be open and creative. She realised that the call to love was linked to the same obedience that brought Jesus to the Cross. Her last months were a painful journey to Jerusalem and to her Calvary. Like Jesus she came to the end in a time of terrible darkness and in this she fulfilled her faithful following, her allegiance to him. By faith she grasped the meaning of the heavenly Jerusalem. Yet at times during her last months she felt as if that reality could be snatched away from her, that her hope might even be in vain. We know that she kept journeying and in the end peace broke through the darkness and the pain.

However, the great contribution, the message that Thérèse has for us today, is of the self-sacrificing love that Christ has for his community, which we learn in a special way by attentive listening to God's word in the Bible. By her life Thérèse

The National Shrine of Saint Thérèse at Darien, Illinois, U.S.A.

became an icon of that love and shows us a face of the Church that is more than the institution. The Carmelite writer Chris O'Donnell is influenced by the theology of Hans Urs von Balthasar when he says that Thérèse has something vital to teach the post-Vatican II Church. If we want a renewed and missionary Church we need to move away from mere organisational and structural change and live love. We will then see the wonderful reality of the Communion of Saints and learn to understand how much worth there is in an act of pure love – in living the 'Little Way'. In her discipleship Thérèse is in many ways a wonderful window into the faith of Mary, whose unconditional trust lived through Calvary and then experienced the fullness of the Resurrection.

The *Letter to the Ephesians* speaks of all of us as 'God's work of art' (2:10). Thérèse is an immortal diamond, crafted by love in her suffering and in her creative way of living life. She was strongly inserted in the Carmelite tradition, living the *Rule of Saint Albert*, and loving the Scriptures. Like the prophet Elijah, she too journeyed to her own meeting with God. Like the prophet, she came to the end of her tether, yet was fed and enabled to carry on. As we read in the Bible's *Books of the Kings*, the prophet encountered God in the Wadi Cherith and on Mount Horeb. Thérèse journeyed with Christ and came to the eternal Mount Sion and the New Jerusalem.

Thérèse and her sisters meditating in the Lourdes Grotto recreated at Lisieux Carmel (1894).

This article is adapted from Wilfrid McGreal, *At the Fountain of Elijah – The Carmelite Tradition*, Traditions of Christian Spirituality Series, (London: Darton, Longman and Todd, 1999), pp. 86-94.

Saint Thérèse depicted in stained glass
at St. Mary's Church, Westport, Co. Mayo, Ireland.

Back to the Gospel
The Message of St. Thérèse of Lisieux

Joseph Chalmers, O.Carm. & Camilo Maccise, O.C.D.

A letter from the O.Carm and O.C.D. Superiors General
on the occasion of the centenary of the death of St. Thérèse of Lisieux
Rome, 16th July 1996, Feast of Our Lady of Mount Carmel

Dear brothers and sisters in Carmel,

1. We will shortly begin to celebrate the centenary of the death of our sister Thérèse of Lisieux. As this anniversary approaches, many are turning their eyes to this young Carmelite, who was a member of a Teresian convent in France and who, in her writings, shared her profound vision of the relationship between God and humankind – the fruit of her personal experience under the guidance of the Holy Spirit.

2. Thérèse's mission was to remind us of the essence of the Christian message: that God is love, and that he gives himself gratuitously to those who are evangelically poor; that holiness is not the fruit of our own efforts, but of divine action, which requires nothing more of us that loving surrender to God's saving grace. Thus her teachings have lost none of their relevance over the years; indeed, their influence has been so great that more than thirty Episcopal Conferences and thousands of Christians have requested that Thérèse be declared a Doctor of the Church.

An evangelical and contemplative woman

3. Although Thérèse of Lisieux spent her religious life in an enclosed Carmelite convent, she was declared Patron of the Missions, because in her, contemplative spirituality was united with its apostolic dimension. She communicated her evangelical experience in language that was both simple and vital, in words that could be understood and absorbed by believers from every country and every culture. Her return to the Gospels and to the Word of God, to the Jesus of history and to the paschal mystery of his death and resurrection, anticipated the Second

Vatican Council. She stressed the priority of love in the Church, the Body of Christ. She bore witness to the spirituality of ordinary life and to the universal call to holiness.

4.   Thérèse's experience and doctrine acquire special meaning in our time, when new possibilities for presence and action in society and in the Church are opening to women. Women are called to be 'a sign of God's tender love for the human race',[1] and to enrich humanity through their 'feminine Genius'. By her life and her writings, our sister did both.

A new look at Thérèse's message

5.   Rereading Thérèse's works from our own social and ecclesial contexts, and from within our own cultural realities, will help us to focus on what is truly essential: trusting openness to God our Father, who loves us and understands us; allegiance to Jesus our brother, who is the way, the truth, and the life, always present and close to us; and obedience to the Holy Spirit, who guides history – our own and that of our religious families. All of this must take place within the acceptance of our own poverty and weakness, with the certainty that nothing can ever separate us from the love of God in Christ Jesus (cf. *Romans* 8:37-39).

6.   We hope that our reflections will help to keep alive the dynamic spirit of this celebration, which must be a time of special grace for all Carmelites – religious, priests and laity.

Present importance of Thérèse to the Church

7.   During the Synod on Consecrated Life [1994], several members of the Synod mentioned our sister as someone who has an important message for the Church at the dawning of the third millennium. Among those who spoke of her in their contributions was the Secretary General, Cardinal Schotte, who concluded his report with the following words:

---

1   *Vita Consecrata* 57. In this text the following abbreviations are used for Church documents: VC = *Vita Consecrata*; GS = *Gaudium et Spes*; DV = *Dei Verbum*; Rule = *The Carmelite Rule* (the opportunity has been taken in this publication to update the paragraph numbering of the *Rule* references according to the system agreed in 1999 between the Ancient and Discalced observances of the Carmelite Family).

In conclusion, may I recall a woman who was an excellent witness to the consecrated life in the mission of the Church: St. Thérèse of the Child Jesus ... This Carmelite nun of Lisieux distinguished herself by her humility, her evangelical simplicity and her trust in God ... In her autobiography she wrote: *As I desired martyrdom intensely, I found an answer in St. Paul's letters. The Apostle explains that the greatest charisms are of no avail without love, and that this very same love is the most certain path to God. And I found peace ... I would be love in the heart of my Mother, the Church.*

8. At an audience on 4th January 1995, Pope John Paul II spoke of the commitment to prayer in consecrated life, and pointed to the importance of prayer for evangelisation. He concluded thus:

    On this point, it seems right to conclude this catechesis with a word about St. Thérèse, who by her prayers and sacrifices contributed to evangelisation just as much as, and perhaps more than she would have, had she been involved in missionary activities – so much so that she was proclaimed Patron of the Missions.[2]

9. The post-synodal apostolic exhortation *Vita Consecrata* also mentions our sister: it speaks of her yearning to be love in the heart of the Church,[3] and her desire to be involved in a unique collaboration with missionary action. She repeatedly expressed her desire to love Jesus and to make him loved[4] through her own communion with him: 'To be your bride, O Jesus ... to be, in union with you, a mother of souls.'[5]

An invitation to focus on the essential

10. In her religious name – Thérèse of the Child Jesus and the Holy Face – our sister summarised her entire life's journey which took her to spiritual maturity through a process of *kenosis*, the self-emptying of the incarnation and the suffering of Jesus, who by his paschal mystery liberates us from every form of slavery. She was able to understand and to live out Jesus's plan of life, through which he transforms the

---

2   *L'Osservatore Romano,* 5th January 1995, p. 4.
3   VC 46.
4   VC 47.
5   VC n. 72.

entire world of our relationships and gives a new dimension to our relationships with God, with others and with all things. Against the *plan of death* which dominates and enslaves us in all these areas, the Gospel offers *a plan of life* which liberates and transforms us. Thérèse's mission was to remind us of these truths, and to centre us again in what is essential.

11. We shall look more carefully at Thérèse's message in the perspective of Jesus's plan of life, which we shall summarise briefly. Her message invites us to pass from the image of God-as-judge to that of God, Father-Mother; from lack of trust to self-abandoned trust in God; from the quest for perfection to the quest for communion with God; from complexity to simplicity; from laws that enslave us to the law of real and effective love which liberates us; from immaturity to maturity; from external asceticism to evangelical selflessness; from trying to earn God's love to standing before him empty-handed; from purely

A sculpture at the National Shrine of St. Thérèse in Darien, Illinois, U.S.A., depicting Thérèse before Christ and his Mother Mary.

spiritual considerations to the Word of God; from complicated prayer to a simple contemplative gaze; from an unreachable Mary to the Mary of the gospels, who is very near to us.

I. JESUS'S PLAN OF LIFE

12. The gospel of Jesus Christ, the Good News he came to bring us, is the proclamation of *life* and of *freedom*. The *freedom* he brings is synonymous with love – a love which forgets itself and gives itself for the good of others.

13. Both in his life on earth and in his teachings, Jesus fulfilled his commitment to life, even to the point of accepting the process of death which culminated in the cross. By his incarnation, Jesus assumed the human condition and gave it its full dignity. Out of this grew his respect for the life of each person and his will to struggle against all that oppresses or diminishes life. He was never insensitive or indifferent to suffering or death. By his attitude, he revealed God's plan, which is a plan of life. Even suffering is, within this plan, a path of life and of resurrection.

14. The God of life made himself present in Jesus of Nazareth. He, who was the Word of life (Jn 1:4), came to give us life in abundance (cf. Jn 10:10), and to transform us into the children of God (Jn 1:14). In the temple in Nazareth, when he began to proclaim the Good News of life, Jesus presented it as liberation (Lk 4:17-21). In this discourse, summing up his mission, he pointed out various forms of enslavement and oppression which control human existence and keep it in a state of death.

15. The plan of life which Jesus presented and initiated affects all three spheres of human relationships: relationships with God, with others, and with all things.

1. From fatalism to the responsibility of children of God

16. To the plan of death, which presented God as the powerful and fearsome creator, Jesus opposed his own plan of life, revealing God as the Father-

Mother who, far from imposing a destiny on us, helps us to overcome fatalism and to cooperate with him freely and responsibly. According to Jesus, our relationship with the God of life is a relationship of love and trust.

17. Jesus revealed to us the face of the Father, and this revelation is the core and the cornerstone of every believer's life, becoming the very centre of existence. The God that Jesus reveals to us is a God who respects our freedom. He is an unknown God who reveals himself in his incarnated Son, and who, through the action of the Spirit, destroys our idols – a God who becomes, more and more fully, the one foundation of our existence.

18. Our commitment to life in all of its dimensions can become reality if it is rooted in this image of the God of Our Lord Jesus Christ.

2. From division to fraternal communion

19. In the plan of life presented and initiated by Jesus, relationships with others are summarised in the commandment to love our neighbour, based on the commandment to love God with all our hearts, our souls and our strength (cf. Mt 27:37-39).

20. Guided by this love, Jesus places himself on the side of the excluded and the marginalised, those condemned to various kinds of death: the poor, the sick, women, children, sinners, strangers. He offers life to them all. He struggles against all that opposes life, as he struggles against all that creates division — between neighbour and stranger, between pagan and Jew, between man and woman.

21. Each human being is a synthesis of creation, accomplished in and by the Word (see Col 1:15-16; Jn 1:3). Because of this, human beings possess a sacred quality which comes to them from God. In the light of Christ, human beings appear in the universe as those who hear the word of God and dialogue with God. By his incarnation, the son of God 'has in a certain way united himself with each human being'.[6] As Matthew's Gospel tells us (Mt 25:31-46), Christ is very near to us,

---

6   GS 22.

present in every human being, 'and with particular tenderness he chose to identify himself with those who are poorest and weakest.'[7]

22. This is a sacramental presence, which at once reveals and conceals. In the face of every human being we can see something of the face of Jesus, the Word of life. We first intuit the mystery of God within our own unique experience and within the autonomous and reciprocal reality of man and of woman. Pope John Paul II has emphasised the dignity of women and their "specific contribution to the Church's life and to pastoral and missionary activity ... The Church depends on ... women for new efforts ... especially in (fostering) everything that affects the dignity of women and respect for human life ... and promoting the fundamental values of life and peace".[8]

23. The discovery of God's presence in others brings about a change in human relationships. It motivates us to live our commitment to love that is real and effective. It demands an openness to universal fraternity in the Church and in society and it invites us to commit ourselves to all that implies life, communion and participation, from the perspective of a preferential option for the poor in whom the face of God is 'dimmed and even defiled'.[9]

3. From a selfish to a shared use of resources

24. In Jesus's plan of life, relationships with material things are transformed. We are invited to move from using things in a way which alienates and enslaves us — leading to the oppression of others, forcing them into various forms of death — to using them with freedom, and, above all, to sharing them with others in a society which is just and human to everyone. For Jesus, material things are places of encounter with God and with our brothers and sisters, means of communication and of communion among people.

25. Jesus's religious message has social implications which result in a commitment to justice as a source of life. This is the expression of the

---

7 Puebla Document (Third General Conference of the Latin American Episcopate held at Puebla de los Angeles, Mexico, 1979), 196.
8 VC 57-58.
9 Puebla Document 1142.

Thérèse depicted in stained glass at the Ermitage centre in Lisieux.

social and communal dimension of his commandment to love. Jesus's plan of life, the Kingdom of God which he announced, has repercussions for the structures within which human beings live together. When these structures are founded on injustice and oppression they become instruments of death. Christ's teachings question and challenge us powerfully on this point, and invite us to commit ourselves to a life of justice.

II. THÉRÈSE OF LISIEUX LIVED AND BORE WITNESS TO JESUS'S PLAN

26.   The celebration of our sister's centenary is a time to re-read her life and her writings in the context of Jesus's project of life, from the perspective of our social, cultural and ecclesial environment. However, reflection on her spiritual experience demands from us, above all, a deep renewal of our lives as Carmelites. Thérèse reminds us of the fundamental values of the Gospel and invites us to centre our lives in them. Reading and meditating the word of God, she discovered the essential aspects of our relationships with him, with others, and with all things; she lived these with great simplicity, deeply and spontaneously, and she communicated them by her life and in her writings.

1. A close and loving God

Drinking from the living source of the Word of God

27.   Thérèse of Lisieux nourished her life and her spirituality from the pure source of the word of God. At a time when reading the Bible was seldom encouraged, she did what the Second Vatican Council would later ask of all believers, and in particular of religious: she acquired 'the surpassing knowledge of Jesus Christ by frequent reading of the divine Scriptures: *Ignorance of the Scriptures is ignorance of Christ*'.[10]

28.   Faithful to the *Rule*, Thérèse meditated day and night on the law of the Lord, and kept watch in prayer.[11] Like her spiritual mother Teresa of Jesus, she found in Jesus a living book[12]; and in imitation of St. John

---

10   DV 25.
11   Cf. *Rule* 10.
12   See Teresa of Jesus, *The Book of Her Life*, 26:5.

of the Cross, she 'fixed her eyes on Christ'.[13] She herself tells us how, little by little, she left spiritual books, which – especially St. John of the Cross – had been of great assistance to her on her journey, and focused on the Scriptures, in particular on the gospels:

> Later on, however, all books left me in aridity. ... If I open a book composed by a spiritual author ... I feel my heart contract immediately and I read without understanding. Or if I do understand, my mind comes to a standstill without the capacity of meditating. In this helplessness, Holy Scripture and the Imitation come to my aid; in them I discover a solid and very pure nourishment. But it is especially the Gospels which sustain me during my hours of prayer, for in them I find what is necessary for my poor little soul. I am constantly discovering in them new lights, hidden and mysterious meanings. I understand and I know from experience that 'The kingdom of God is within us'.[14]

29.   Reading and reflecting on the Word of God, Thérèse discovered the essence of Jesus's message in ordinary daily life. This link between the Word of God and concrete everyday life led her 'to find, just when I need them, certain lights which I had not seen until then ... in the midst of my daily occupations.'[15] But it is primarily in his liberating Word that Jesus made himself present to Thérèse: 'Never have I heard him speak, but I feel that he is within me at each moment, guiding me, and inspiring what I must say and do.'[16]

30.   In her efforts to remind us of the essential, Thérèse presents the Word of God as a lamp which sheds light on our paths (cf. Ps 119:105).[17] She reminds us that in order to understand God's message, we must have the hearts of children open and available to whatever the Spirit is saying to us and asking of us in our vocations and in our mission in the Church.

31.   We need to be constantly attentive to the word of God, 'the source of all Christian spirituality.'[18] The Church recommends communal meditation

---

13 John of the Cross, *Ascent of Mount Carmel*, II Ch 22:5.
14 *Story of a Soul*, VIII (Manuscript A, 83v); cf. 1992 *Catechism of the Catholic Church*, 127.
15 *Ibid.*
16 *Ibid.*
17 Cf. *Story of a Soul*, X (Manuscript C 4r).
18 VC 94.

on the Bible, not only for consecrated people, but for all members of the People of God. 'From familiarity with God's word, they draw the light needed for the individual and communal discernment which helps them to seek the ways of the Lord in the signs of the times.'[19]

32.   Thérèse of Lisieux, whose devotion to the Scriptures was so great that she wanted to learn the biblical languages in order to enjoy the word of God better, was not in contact with the recent Church approach to the Scriptures. Nor did her environment give her the opportunities we have today to acquire better knowledge and understanding of the biblical message. Nonetheless, she practised the Carmelite *Rule*'s recommendation to keep the word of God abundantly on her lips, and in her heart, so that all that she did might always be in agreement with the word.[20] Let us read and meditate the word of God, as our sister did, and let us put its demands into practice, using the new means that God offers us, at this particular time in the history of the Church, to assist us in deepening our understanding of his word.

Rediscovering the paternal-maternal face of God

33.   Thérèse lived in an era characterised by a Jansenist spirituality which deformed the face of God, presenting him exclusively as a severe judge who could even ask us to offer ourselves as victims in an effort to appease his wrath.

34.   In reading and meditating upon the word of God, Thérèse of Lisieux opened her heart to Jesus, who revealed to her the true face of God: the merciful father-mother who invites us to live as his sons and daughters, in trust and in self-abandonment, surrendering ourselves to divine love, assuming with responsibility – as Christ did – the mission to proclaim God's plan for humanity. She understood 'how Jesus wants to be loved', and she offered herself as a sacrifice to his all-merciful Love, which wishes to communicate itself to all people.[21]

---

19 *Ibid.* 94.
20 Cf. *Rule* 19.
21 *Story of a Soul*, VIII (Manuscript A, 83v).

Prayer as simple filial dialogue

35.   Like her spiritual mother Teresa of Avila,[22] Thérèse of Lisieux experienced prayer as a trusting and loving dialogue with God the Father-Mother.[23] The strength which comes from prayer opened her to the evangelical abnegation necessary for authentic prayer, and was transformed into vital experience. 'It is prayer, it is sacrifice which give me all my strength; these are the invincible weapons which Jesus has given me. They can touch souls much better than words.'[24]

Her prayer became increasingly simple, placing her at the very source of the living water, in the divine fire which purifies and transforms. 'For me, prayer is a surge of the heart, it is a simple look turned toward heaven, it is a cry of recognition and of love, embracing both trial and joy; it is something great, supernatural, which expands my soul and unites me with Jesus.'[25]

From holiness as 'perfection' to holiness as communion

36.   For Thérèse, the rediscovery of the paternal and maternal face of God marked the beginning of a new path towards holiness. She followed this path most fully after the onset of her illness in 1894. As she tells us in her writings, Jesus showed her that the way to holiness lies in the trust and self-abandonment of a child who falls asleep without fear in the arms of his Father:

> *'Whoever is a little one, let him come to me.'* So speaks the Holy Spirit through the mouth of Solomon. This same Spirit of Love also says: *'For to him that is little, mercy will be shown.'* The prophet Isaiah reveals in His name that on the last day ... *'as a mother comforts her child, so I will comfort you; I shall carry you at my breasts, and caress you on my knees'* ... Jesus does not demand great actions from us but simply surrender and gratitude.[26]

---

22 See Teresa of Jesus, *The Book of her Life*, Ch. 8:5: 'For mental prayer, in my opinion, is nothing else than an intimate sharing between friends; it means taking time frequently to be alone with him who we know loves us.'

23 Cf. Teresa of Jesus, *The Book of her Life*, Ch. 8:5; *The Way of Perfection*, Ch. 31:9.

24 *Story of a Soul*, XI (Manuscript C, 24v).

25 *Story of a Soul*, XI (Manuscript C, 25r-v). This definition of prayer opens the section on Prayer in the 1992 *Catechism of the Catholic Church*, 2559.

26 *Story of a Soul*, IX (Manuscript B, 1r-v).

37. This is the transition from fear to trust. We stand before God as children before a father and a mother. God makes everything, even our faults and our mistakes, work for our good:

> It is confidence and nothing but confidence that must lead us to Love ... What pleases him is that he sees me loving my littleness and my poverty, the blind hope that I have in his mercy ... To love Jesus, to be his victim of love – the weaker one is, without desires or virtues, the more suited one is for the workings of this consuming and transforming Love.[27]

38. At the root of our vocation to consecrated life in Carmel is the Lord's initiative. In responding to God's invitation, those who have been called entrust themselves to his love, dedicating their lives unconditionally to God, 'consecrating to him all things present and future, and placing them in his hands.'[28] Like Thérèse of Lisieux, we are called to live profoundly the experience of the paternal and maternal face of God; to experience prayer as a loving dialogue with God and as a contemplative look at reality, an attentive ear turned to God as we commit ourselves to our brothers and sisters; to look at holiness not as 'perfection' but as communion with God in faith, hope, and love – the sanctity of the theological virtues laid out in the *Rule* and St. John of the Cross, who through his writings was Thérèse's teacher and spiritual father.

Fidelity to our mission and purification of our faith

39. The gratuitous experience of the paternal and maternal face of God, revealed in Jesus, and fidelity to one's own vocation and mission, responsibility assumed as sons and daughters of God, enter into the dynamic of the paschal mystery of death and resurrection. They are subject to purification and to the test of faith. Thérèse of Lisieux expressed this by adding to her name, in an inseparable unity, 'the Child Jesus' and 'the Holy Face'. The incarnated Word who, in the mystery of his childhood, invites us to trust, to love and to abandonment, is the same suffering servant who introduces us to the mysterious path which he himself trod before us – a suffering arising from fidelity to the Father's mission.

27 *Letter* 197, to Sr. Marie of the Sacred Heart, 17th September 1896.
28 VC 17.

40.   Thérèse discovered and understood her vocation through a process of purification of her faith in God. Her apostolic yeaning to proclaim the Good News of salvation became a martyrdom of love, as she could see no way to combine or realise all of her desires. God led her to understand, in the light of Chapters 12 and 13 of the *First Letter to the Corinthians*, that the Church is like a body, and that in this body love is the heart which sets in motion all the other parts and which, for this reason, encompasses all vocations, regardless of age and place. When Thérèse understood this, she exclaimed: 'My vocation – at last I have found it – my vocation is love! Yes, I have found my place in the Church and it is You, O my God, who have given me this place; in the heart of the Church, my mother, I shall be love! Thus I shall be everything, and thus my dream will be realised!'[29]

41.   What has been described as *St Thérèse of Lisieux's passion*[30] can be seen powerfully in her *Last Conversations*. This passion was an experience of purifying darkness, of illness, shadow, doubts and pangs of death. In her efforts to be faithful to her contemplative vocation, she followed the path to Calvary: 'At that time I had many great interior trials of all sorts (I even wondered at times whether heaven existed).'[31] In the last months of her life, this purifying darkness became particularly dense. Thérèse drank the cup of pain to its very dregs. Like Jesus, she offered her life for others.

42.   The paschal dimension of consecrated life also includes the cross and suffering, in fidelity to the fulfilment of the commitment to the Church's mission;[32] for 'a sense of mission is essential to every Institute, not only those dedicated to the active apostolic life, but also those dedicated to the contemplative life. Indeed, more than in external works, the mission consists in making Christ present to the world through personal witness.'[33]

        In the fulfilment of our mission, we are called, like Thérèse of Lisieux, to experience the purification of our faith – the shield that protects us from the temptations of evil.[34] In times of hardship, including

29 *Story of a Soul*, IX (Manuscript B, 3v).
30 Title of a book by Guy Gaucher, O.C.D.
31 *Story of a Soul*, VIII (Manuscript A, 80v).
32 Cf. VC 24.
33 *Ibid*. 72.
34 Cf. *Rule* 19.

persecution and martyrdom, we are called to assume the cross as 'the superabundance of God's love poured out upon this world ... the great sign of Christ's saving presence, especially in the midst of difficulties and trials.'[35]

2. A God who builds community

The evangelical dimensions of fraternal love

43.   The second aspect of Jesus's plan is overcoming hatred and division, in order to achieve love and communion with all those to whom he calls us. This call is closely linked to the discovery of the paternal and maternal face of God which, in Christ, has transformed us into brothers and sisters. This is the second part of the one commandment of love: to love our neighbour as we love ourself.

44.   In Thérèse of Lisieux's experience and doctrine we find the conviction that the authenticity of our love for God is manifested in the quality of our love for our neighbour. The dimension of fraternal love gradually expands to encompass wider and wider horizons, in a series of concentric circles – an expansion which has its source in the love of God. The first circle holds those who are closest to us; the largest one encompasses the entire human race. For Thérèse, trust and abandonment to God the Father-Mother, and the knowledge of being loved by him, are the source of fraternal charity and of apostolate – the expression of love for all human beings in the desire to share with them the good news of salvation.

Fraternal love and life in community

45.   We live the evangelical dimensions of fraternal love through the concrete realities of our human existence: family, religious community, Christian communities, Church, various groups and associations, society as a whole. In each of these we encounter light and darkness, positive and negative aspects. Thérèse teaches us to be a living part of this reality and to begin living evangelical love wherever God has placed us.

---

35 VC 24.

46. When Thérèse entered the Carmelite convent in Lisieux it was, in the words of her sister Marie, a small and poor convent. There were 26 religious; the average age was 47. It was a poor community in human terms, and spiritually it was influenced both by the rigorous attitudes of the time and by fear of an avenging God, the legacy of Jansenism. All this created a continual obstacle to the dynamism of love and balance which St. Teresa of Jesus sought to protect by her spiritual and human realism. In this environment, among real people – people with names, qualities and faults – Thérèse of Lisieux lived out fraternal love and responded to its demands.

47. Many passages in Manuscript C [of *Story of a Soul*], addressed to Mother Marie de Gonzaga, Prioress of the convent, describe Thérèse's gradual progress in understanding and living Jesus's commandment to love others as he loved us. She learned to tolerate the faults of others; not to be alienated by their weaknesses, to learn from small signs of virtue; to judge everyone with understanding and kindness. The manuscript also describes a few specific incidents which put her love for others to the test and set obstacles in the path of communion.[36] In the small efforts, services and sacrifices of fraternal life in community, Thérèse lived the precept of love.

48. The dimension of communion which is an integral part of the vocation to consecrated life, stressed also in our *Rule*, has been recently emphasised by *Vita Consecrata* in the second part entitled *Signum fraternitatis: Consecrated life as a sign of communion in the Church.*[37]

    The paschal mystery helps us to understand that without renunciation, without the cross, without generous devotion, openness and forgiveness, we cannot love others as Jesus did. Thérèse of Lisieux teaches and inspires us to live the new communion and fraternity in Christ within the concrete circumstances of our communities, in the midst of all our difficulties.

---

36 Cf. *Story of a Soul*, X-XI (Manuscript C, 11v-22v).
37 Earlier, in February 1994, the Congregation for Institutes of Consecrated Life and Societies of Apostolic Life published a document on *Fraternal Life in Community*, which contains concrete and realistic directions for growth and development, as families gathered in the name of the Lord.

3. A God who asks us to announce the Good News

The missionary dimension: to love Jesus and to make him loved

49.   Commitment to evangelisation is an expression of universal love. To witness to others the new life in Christ and to proclaim Christ's message of hope, is to love them. In her life as a contemplative nun, Thérèse never ceased to live the missionary and apostolic dynamic of the Christian vocation. From her particular vocation to Carmel, she wanted to cooperate with Christ in the redemption of the world – not only until the end of her life, but until the end of time.[38]

    In her letters to her missionary brothers, she emphasised in many ways the apostolic and missionary dimension of the contemplative Carmelite life. Among other things, she stated: 'You know that a Carmelite who would not be an apostle would separate herself from the goal of her vocation and would cease to be a daughter of the Seraphic Saint Teresa, who desired to give a thousand lives to save a single soul.'[39] She therefore wanted to live every vocation,[40] but the effectiveness of evangelisation required her simply to fulfil the task of love; and she begged the saints to obtain for her twice their capacity for love.[41]

50.   We have been called to Carmel, and therefore have been consecrated for mission. We have 'the prophetic task of recalling and serving the divine plan for humanity, as it is announced in Scripture and as it emerges from an attentive reading of the signs of God's providential action in history. This is the plan for the salvation and reconciliation of humanity.'[42] From our sister Thérèse, we must learn the apostolic orientation of our Christian love; faith in the evangelising power of prayer; and the need for a spirituality that is incarnated in the realities of everyday life. Evangelisation is not merely information.

    As children of God, we grow in love and in solidarity; evangelisation is the manifestation of this. We are called to experience, and to assume from this perspective, the pain and the anguish of our brothers and

---

38   cf. *Story of a Soul*, IX (Manuscript B, 3r).
39   *Letter* 198 to the Abbé Maurice Bellière, 21st October 1896.
40   Cf. *Story of a Soul*, IX (Manuscript B, 2v).
41   Cf. *Story of a Soul*, IX (Manuscript B, 4r).
42   VC 73.

sisters. Thérèse accepted the trial of experiencing the doubts of unbelievers in order to obtain for them the grace of overcoming these doubts. She sat at the table of sinners and of those who refuse faith, and she suffered with them in their emptiness and in their darkness: 'Your child ... begs pardon for her brothers. She accepts to eat the bread of sorrow as long as you desire it; she does not wish to rise from this table filled with bitterness, at which poor sinners are eating, until the day set by you.'[43] This, too, is a way of offering a spiritual response to the search for the sacred and to the longing for God which is always present in the human heart.[44]

51. This love also has a social dimension which obliges us, in the many ways that are specific to each vocation within the Carmelite family, to a service of integral promotion, fostering justice and peace throughout the world by means of the authentic human development of all people. To be effective, love for others must be expressed in a way that is coherent with the needs of the contemporary world. Thus we are called to have a social aspect in our love because each day the means of expressing individual love are shrinking. Our neighbour in need is not the isolated individual, but rather the masses oppressed by unjust and dehumanising structures.

There is an urgent need for the presence of Christian love in the work of transforming and changing structures. Charity is stronger than divisions. In the struggle for a more just world, it helps us to overcome hatred which would in the end turn the oppressed into the oppressor. Only the love of Jesus, and the testimony of his life and of his doctrine, can lead to true fraternal reconciliation. The doctrine of the path of spiritual childhood is a tremendous force for social change in the face of the abuses of power in society.

Close to Mary of Nazareth

52. For us, Mary is the model of consecration and of discipleship, reminding us of the primacy of God's initiative and teaching us to accept grace. She teaches us 'unconditional discipleship and diligent

---

43 *Story of a Soul*, X (Manuscript C, 6r).
44 cf. VC 103.

service'.[45] In keeping with the purest Carmelite tradition, Thérèse of Lisieux lived in the close presence of the Mother of Jesus. Long before the Second Vatican Council, she discovered the simple woman of Nazareth, pilgrim of faith and of hope, Mother and model. She can be said to have lived her life by Mary's side.

53.   Thérèse rejected those images of Mary which exalt her greatness without taking her earthly life into account: 'For a sermon on the Blessed Virgin to please me and do me any good, I must see her real life, not her imagined life. I am sure that her real life was very simple. Preachers show her to us as unapproachable, but they should present her as imitable, bringing out her virtues, saying that she lived by faith just like ourselves ... She is more Mother than Queen.'[46]

Thérèse's last poem, dedicated to Mary, is titled *Why I love you, Mary*. It is a journey through the pages of the gospel, where Thérèse discovered Mary's love for God and for others, her poverty, her contemplative silence, her simplicity, her faith, her hope, her receptivity and obedience in accepting the will of God. The gospel tells us who Mary was, and Thérèse's heart revealed to her, in her experience of daily life in communion with the Virgin, Mary's true personality.[47]

54.   In the teachings of Thérèse of Lisieux, we find a path which leads us to a deepened and renewed Marian life, in the light of the gospel and of intimacy with Mary. The rediscovery of Mary, in the mystery of Christ and of the Church, gives a more solid base to our devotion, our witness and our preaching. The entire history of our Order, from its earliest days on Mount Carmel, is imbued with Mary's presence.

Above all, Mary is the model of discipleship in faith and contemplation. As Thérèse experienced, Mary teaches us, most of all, the attitudes of Prayer: discernment, availability (the Annunciation); praise and gratitude for all that God does throughout history for the poor and the simple (the Magnificat); faith (the wedding at Cana); patient and contemplative expectation, keeping all things in her heart without the need to understand, until light dawns (finding Jesus in the temple);

---

45 VC 28.
46 *Last Conversations*, 21st August 1897.
47 *Poems*, 49 (p. 152).

fidelity in times of trial (at the foot of the cross); communion and a sense of Church (praying with the disciples).

Prophetic witness in the face of challenge

55.   Christians, and especially those in consecrated life, are called to give prophetic witness by proclaiming the gospel values and denouncing all that is opposed to them. Pope John Paul II, highlighting the prophetic character of consecrated life 'as a special form of sharing in Christ's prophetic office, which the Holy Spirit communicates to the whole People of God', recalled the figure of Elijah, 'courageous prophet and friend of God', as a model of the authentic prophet. In his description of Elijah, John Paul II says that Elijah lived in the presence of the Lord, 'and contemplated his passing-by in silence; he interceded for the people and boldly announced God's will; he ... came to the defence of the poor against the powerful of the world.'[48]

56.   Seen from this perspective, Thérèse can be called a prophet of the new times. She has been described, and with good reason, as the 'prophet of youth'; a 'sign of hope'; the 'prophet of holiness as a vocation offered to everyone'; a 'prophet of the actuality of redemption', emphasising the invisible power of love.[49] Thérèse, whose powerful desires marked her paschal journey, has much to say to a searching and dissatisfied humanity.

In keeping with Carmelite tradition, Thérèse saw the prophet Elijah as a model for life. Not only was she drawn by the prophet's experience of God in the 'gentle breeze'[50] but also by his struggle against the prophets of Baal: 'After having shown us the illustrious origins of our Holy Order, after having compared us to the Prophet Elijah fighting against the priests of Baal, he declared "Times similar to those of Achab's persecution are about to begin again." We seemed to be flying already to martyrdom.'[51]

---

48   VC 84.
49   Cf. Jean-Marie Lustiger, *La petite Thérèse, 'la plus grande sainte des temps modernes': Homélie à Lisieux pour la fête de Sainte Thérèse,* 25th September 1983.
50   Cf. *Story of a Soul,* IV and VIII (Manuscript A 36v; 76v).
51   *Letter* 192 to Mme Guérin, 16th July 1896.

57.   In fidelity to our Carmelite vocation, we are called to bear prophetic witness, through lives that emphasise the primacy of God in the experience of his presence at the heart of the world. We are called to an openness which enables us to discover his presence in ways that are always new and surprising – as Elijah did in the gentle wind – and which will motivate us to commit ourselves to the service of our brothers and sisters to help them in their struggle for integral liberation. Fraternal life 'is itself prophetic in a society which, sometimes without realising it has a profound yearning for a brotherhood which knows no borders.' Moreover, 'prophecy derives a particularly persuasive power from consistency between proclamation and life.'[52]

A living and guiding presence

58.   The evangelical quality of Thérèse of Lisieux's experience and doctrine gives them permanent relevance. The simplicity, the trust, and the abandonment to God which Thérèse lived and proclaimed are capable of inspiring a commitment to justice and peace in the world.[53]

59.   Thérèse's influence on the Church and on the world of today cannot be doubted. She knew this intuitively when she affirmed before dying, 'I feel, especially, that my mission is about to begin, my mission of making God loved as I love him, of giving my little way to souls. If God answers my desires, my heaven will be spent on earth until the end of the world. Yes, I want to spend my heaven in doing good on earth.'[54]

---

52 VC 85.
53 In connection with this, we have the testimony of a North American priest who was imprisoned for protesting against the fact that troops in El Salvador were being trained in the U.S.A. to kill their brothers and sisters. In 1985 he wrote, from his prison cell: 'As a modern soul, struggling for union with God, I feel that the spirituality of St Thérèse (of Lisieux) is as valid today as it was in 1897. A spirituality for all times, for all ages. I wonder what transformation would take place in my own heart, and in the heart of the world, if simplicity, trust and self-surrender to God were taken seriously. The more clearly this 'modern' soul (his own) sees the reality of the modern world he is living in today, the more convincing is St Thérèse's way of seeking union with God and justice and peace in the world.' (Roy Bourgeoise, Maryknoll priest: letter from a federal cell, 1985. Quoted by C. Ackerman and J. Haley, in 'Reinterpreting Thérèse of Lisieux for Today' in *Spiritual Life*, Vol. 35, No. 2, Summer 1989, p. 98).
54 *Last Conversations,* 17th July 1897; Cf. 1992 *Catechism of the Catholic Church,* 956.

Thérèse (left) depicted among the holy men and women of Carmel in a painting at the Carmelite-served parish of Our Lady of Lourdes in Calle Real, El Salvador.

Conclusion

Renewing our contemplative and apostolic life with our sister Thérèse

60.   The centenary of our sister Thérèse's death is an invitation from God to renew ourselves in the light of her experience and her doctrine. As Pope John Paul II said to all religious, we have 'not only a glorious history to remember and to recount, but also a great history still to be accomplished.'[55] We must look to the future, 'where the Spirit is sending us in order to do even greater things.'

Our sister Thérèse points to the path that we must follow – the path of going back to the gospel as the only way to live in true creative fidelity to our charism.

---

55   VC 110.

61.   Thérèse teaches us the central importance of love, which simplifies and communicates the genuine freedom and liberation which lead to a mature Christian, religious and Carmelite identity. In a world filled with anguish and fear, she guides us towards trust and abandonment in the Lord who overcomes all difficulties. To our disembodied idealisms, she opposes a spiritual and evangelical realism, so that we may be true prophets of a God who is present, near and liberating.

As has been pointed out – not only by those consecrated to contemplation, but also by those who work in the field of an evangelisation committed to human growth, development and liberation[56] – Thérèse's message is a challenge to the spirituality of today's Church. Spiritual childhood is an evangelical concept, which implies both awareness of the gift we have received of being sons and daughters of God, and the response that lead us to communion.

62.   Brothers and sisters in Carmel, let us give thanks to the Lord for the gift of our sister Thérèse of Lisieux to the Church, to the world, and to Carmel. Let us experience her presence and her nearness as we celebrate the centenary of her death and as we continue witnessing to the God of our Lord Jesus Christ, in the power of the Holy Spirit.

The Lisieux Carmelite community at recreation in 1895
(Thérèse standing at the left-hand side).

---

56   VC 110.

*A wooden statue of Saint Thérèse by Philip Lindsey Clark
at the Carmelite friary in East Finchley, London.*

Thérèse of Lisieux: Journeying into Weakness

James McCaffrey, O.C.D.

Vatican II anticipated

Thérèse of Lisieux died at the age of twenty-four. One might readily be forgiven for expecting to find little in her writings to better our understanding of the scriptures. Moreover, she was brought up in a narrow and rigid family environment and was not particularly well educated. She was hidden for nine years in an enclosed Carmelite convent, practically unrecognised – even within her own community. She died unknown to the world at large. The milieu in which she lived would appear to be one of intellectual poverty. There had not yet been a Second Vatican Council to restore the word of God to its rightful place at the heart of the Christian life. In her day, the people of God were ill-prepared for the new and challenging insights of our modern approaches to the scriptures.[1] Biblical renewal had hardly begun in earnest. So, we may well ask: has Thérèse anything significant to tell us about the word of God? In fact, her teaching in many ways anticipates some of the richest insights of Vatican II – it explains, deepens, expands and develops them. Both her life and her writings can help us understand better the Council's teaching on the scriptures.

On her deathbed, Thérèse could say, 'Yes, it seems to me I never sought anything but the truth' (LC, p. 205).[2] It is hardly surprising, then, that the Holy Spirit drew Thérèse, in this quest, to the truth of the gospels. Long before Vatican II, she was to discover for herself this lesson of the Council: 'It is common knowledge that among all the Scriptures, even those of the New Testament, the Gospels have a special pre-eminence'.[3] For her, too, the gospels were, in the words of the Council, 'the principal witness of the life and teaching of the incarnate Word, our Saviour'.[4] She once wrote: 'as yet I had not discovered the treasures hidden in the Gospels' (SS, p. 102); but later she could say: 'I have only to cast a glance in the Gospels and immediately I breathe in the perfumes

---

1   For an outline and critical assessment of methods of interpreting the Bible, see Pontifical Biblical Commission, *The Interpretation of the Bible in the Church*, (Vatican: Libreria Editrice Vaticana, 1993), and *The Jewish People and their Sacred Scriptures in the Christian Bible*, (Vatican: Libreria Editrice Vaticana, 2002), especially §19-22, pp. 42-51.
2   References to Thérèse's works and to the books of the Bible are abbreviated; for the full list of abbreviations please see the opening pages of this volume.
3   *Dei Verbum* (*Dogmatic Constitution on Divine Revelation*) 18. This and other official Church documents are printed by the various publishers to the Holy See (Catholic Truth Society, Veritas, etc.). Most such documents can also be consulted on the Vatican's website: www.vatican.va.
4   *Ibid.* 18.

of Jesus' life' (SS, p. 258). Only the gospels could satisfy her fully. She was always discovering in them 'new lights, hidden and mysterious meanings' (SS, p. 179). One sentence says it all: 'with the exception of the Gospels, I no longer find anything in books. The Gospels are enough' (LC, p. 44). It is little wonder that she cries out: 'Show me the secrets hidden in the Gospel. / Ah! that golden book / Is my dearest treasure' (PN 24, stanza 12).

Thérèse was also to discover for herself, as the Council expresses it, 'the true word of God in the books of the Old Testament'.[5] She wrote deeply and movingly of God's mercy and justice. She would not have needed the Council's reminder that the Old Testament reveals 'the ways in which God, just and merciful, deals with people'.[6] It was in the Old Testament that she found reassurance for the truth of her '*little* doctrine' (SS, p. 189): 'Whoever is a *little one*, let him come to me [Pr 9:4]... *For to him that is little, mercy will be shown* [Wis 6:7]... *God shall feed his flock like a shepherd; he shall gather together the lambs with his arm, and shall take them up in his bosom* [Is 40:11]... *As one whom a mother caresses, so will I comfort you; you shall be carried at the breasts and upon the knees they will caress you* [Is 66:13.12]' (SS, p. 188; cf. p. 208). Vatican II stresses the perennial value of the Old Testament, reminding us that 'these books, therefore, written under divine inspiration, remain permanently valuable' and that 'Christians should receive them with reverence'.[7] Thérèse did revere them: 'So speaks the Holy Spirit,' she says, 'through the mouth of Solomon' (SS, p. 188); and she writes a few lines later: 'this same prophet [Isaiah] whose gaze was already plunged into the eternal depths cried out in the Lord's name' (SS, p. 188).

Thérèse the reader

When Thérèse read scripture, she had an eye to detail. She mentions Jesus' '*look of love*' which pierces into the heart of the rich young man (LT 247; cf. Mk 10:21). She draws attention to the '*pillow*' on which Jesus rests his head during the storm at sea, this time observing explicitly: 'The Gospel gives us this detail' (LT 144; cf. Mk 4:38). She reminds us that Jesus, at prayer, gave thanks 'in a transport of joy' to the Father (SS, p. 209; cf. Lk 10:21). Even the presence of Tobias' dog will not escape her observant eye (LT 18a; cf. Tb 11:4). Such minute attention to detail is indeed striking.

We might readily conclude that Thérèse had lots of time for study of the Bible. Nothing could be farther from the truth. For reading, she had at her

---

5   *Ibid.* 14.
6   *Ibid.* 15.
7   *Ibid.* 14-15.

84

disposal half an hour each day, a little longer perhaps on special days.[8] But pressure of work, and her duties with the novices, rarely left her free. Still, she copied and compared, repeated and memorised, meditated and lived the word of God. So close was her intimacy with it that she *became* a 'Word of God'.[9] Many of us today lead busy, tense and often chaotic lives. Thérèse challenges us to plunge ourselves into scripture, however little time we have, however great the pressure. She is an example and inspiration for all of us.

But Thérèse did not just *read* the Bible. She also anticipates the lesson of Vatican II: 'prayer should accompany the reading of sacred Scripture'.[10] And so she writes, 'it is especially the *Gospels* that sustain me during my hours of prayer' (SS, p. 179). The discovery of truth in the word of God, however, did not always come easily to Thérèse. Speaking of the scriptures, she explains: 'this *vast field* seems to us to be a desert, arid and without water... We *know no longer* where *we are*; instead of peace and light, we find only turmoil or at least darkness' (LT 165). Still, she persevered. Even the arid word was a word of life.

Open to new insights

At first sight, it might appear that Thérèse was anti-intellectual in her approach to reading. A casual remark to her sister Céline is often quoted. When they were one day standing in front of a library, Thérèse exclaimed gaily: 'Oh! I would have been sorry to have read all those books!' Céline asked why. She could understand regretting having to read them, but not already having read them. Thérèse explained: 'If I had read them, I would have broken my head, and I would have wasted precious time that I could have employed very simply in loving God' (LC, p. 261). However light-hearted the tone, the point is a serious one. For, as Thérèse wrote to a missionary priest shortly before her death: 'At times, when I am reading certain spiritual treatises in which perfection is shown through a thousand obstacles, surrounded by a crowd of illusions, my poor little mind quickly tires; I close the learned book that is breaking my head

---

8   At the Carmel of Lisieux, half an hour a day was assigned to 'spiritual reading' (2.30-3pm), a time which was, however, also designated for the meeting of the novices. Otherwise, there was one hour's 'free time' during the silence before Matins (8-9pm) and, during the summer when the night's sleep was curtailed, an additional hour in the middle of the day for 'free time' or 'siesta' (12-1pm). See Sainte Thérèse de l'Enfant-Jésus et de la Sainte-Face, *Œuvres complètes*, (Paris: Cerf & Desclée De Brouwer, 1992), pp. 1523-4.

9   An expression used by Pius XI in his Italian discourse of 11th February 1923, quoted in *La Bible avec Thérèse de Lisieux*, compiled by Sr Cécile, O.C.D. & Sr Geneviève, O.P., (Paris: Cerf & Desclée De Brouwer, 1979), p. 40. Edith Stein speaks of Thérèse in the same way: '[her] entire life in the Order was a translation of Sacred Scripture into life': see *Self-Portrait in Letters 1916-1942*, trans. Josephine Koeppel, O.C.D., (Washington, D.C.: I.C.S. Publications, 1993), pp. 218-9 (also p. 219, note 3, which shows that these words almost certainly refer to Thérèse).

10   *Dei Verbum* (*Dogmatic Constitution on Divine Revelation*) 25.

and drying up my heart, and I take up Holy Scripture' (LT 226). But her priority of loving God does not mean abdicating the intellect.

Vatican II has reaffirmed the importance of the study of biblical languages: 'the Church with maternal concern sees to it that suitable and correct translations are made into different languages, especially from the original texts of the sacred books.'[11] The mature Thérèse would have embraced this teaching: 'Had I been a priest, I would have learned Hebrew and Greek,' she said wistfully, 'and wouldn't have been satisfied with Latin. In this way, I would have known the real text dictated by the Holy Spirit' (LC, p. 132). She chose carefully between this or that translation and confessed that she was 'sad to see so many different translations' (LC, p. 132). She felt a need to know the exact meaning of the original biblical terms. We know that Thérèse tried to harmonise the resurrection texts of all four gospels.[12] We have to admire the seriousness of her work. It was a minute, careful and painstaking task. In her day, making a gospel harmony – which today we know to be quite impossible – was common practice among biblical experts; even her own novice would later put together a harmony of the gospels.[13] Thérèse's attempt shows that she was open to the scholarly approach and prepared to try it herself.

Thérèse depicted in stained glass by the artist Frances Biggs at Terenure Carmelite College, Dublin.

11 *Ibid.* 22.
12 For the full text of this harmony, see *La Bible, op. cit.*, pp. 183-5.
13 See Pierre Descouvemont, *Thérèse of Lisieux and Marie of the Trinity: The Transformative Relationship of Saint Thérèse of Lisieux and her Novice Sister Marie of the Trinity*, (New York: Alba House, 1997), p. 44.

To the heart of the gospels[14]

Thérèse seems to have discovered for herself that each evangelist has his own particular slant in his portrait of Jesus. Mark's Jesus is the Suffering Messiah – weak, rejected and misunderstood even by his own disciples. Generally speaking, we are closer in *Mark* to the historical Jesus than in any of the other gospels. Thérèse focuses repeatedly on his scene of Jesus with the disciples in the storm-tossed boat (Mk 4:35-41).[15] Here, she finds a Jesus after her own heart who fully accepts the human condition. He is weak, tired and eminently human. But Thérèse will also interpret the scene with her own original touch: 'Living on Love, when Jesus is sleeping, / Is rest on stormy seas. / Oh! Lord, don't fear that I'll wake you. / I'm waiting in peace for Heaven's shore' (PN 17, stanza 9). She will not disturb him. He can sleep on and take his rest until eternity dawns. She decides he will get weary of waiting for her before she grows tired of waiting for him.

One small incident helps us to see how Thérèse penetrates to the core of Jesus' message in *Matthew* also. A few weeks before she died, she asked her sister to read the Sunday gospel for her. 'I didn't have the missal,' comments Pauline, 'and told her simply: "It's the Gospel where Our Lord warns us against serving two masters." Then, imitating the voice of a little child reciting her lesson by heart, she said it from memory from beginning to end' (LC, pp. 188-9). A significant warning runs through the passage like a refrain: 'Do not be anxious about your life... do not be anxious about tomorrow, let tomorrow take care of itself' (Mt 6:25.34). It contains the kernel of her 'Little Way' of surrender and confidence.

Luke, in turn, is the gospel of God's mercy. His Jesus is the compassionate and merciful Saviour, with the message that 'repentance and forgiveness of sins should be preached in his name to all nations' (Lk 24:47). Thérèse echoes the central message of his gospel: 'I don't hasten to the first place but to the last; rather than advance like the Pharisee, I repeat, filled with confidence, the publican's humble prayer. Most of all I imitate the conduct of Madgalene; her astonishing or rather her loving audacity which charms the Heart of Jesus also attracts my own... I know how much He loves the prodigal child who returns to Him' (SS, pp. 258-9). All these gospel characters are found in *Luke*. The first words of Thérèse's life story express admirably the purpose of his gospel: 'I

---

14 See the author's *Prayer: the Heart of the Gospels*, (Dublin: Columba Press, 2008), and, for a brief synthesis of prayer in the gospels, his *A Biblical Prayer Journey in the Holy Land*, (Burgos: Editorial Monte Carmelo, 1998), pp. 310-22.
15 For a complete list of texts, see *La Bible*, *op. cit.*, pp. 187-90.

shall begin to sing what I must sing eternally: *"The Mercies of the Lord"'* (SS, p. 13; cf. p. 205).

So, too, Thérèse pierces straight to the heart of John's gospel: 'It seems to me that the *word* of Jesus is *Himself*... He, *Jesus*, the *Word*, the *Word* of *God!*' Then she reminds us how 'Jesus teaches us that He is the way, the *truth*, the life' (LT 165). This is John's special slant on the mystery of Jesus. He is the Word: the revelation in person of the Father, 'full of grace and truth' (Jn 1:14) – that is, full of God's enduring and merciful love. This is the love to which Thérèse offers herself as a victim of holocaust, 'until the shadows having disappeared I may be able to tell You of my *Love* in an *Eternal Face to Face!*' (SS, p. 277).

A free and easy approach

In her approach to the Bible, Thérèse is uninhibited. She will not hesitate to fuse texts, even from different gospels. She asks a question in the words of *John*, 'Master, where do you live?', and replies with a variation of *Luke*: 'I [Jesus] have no place to rest my head' (LT 137; cf. Jn 1:38; Lk 9:58). She recalls the words of the fourth gospel, 'Lift up your eyes and see how the fields are already white enough to be harvested', but then continues in the words of *Matthew*: 'the harvest is abundant but the number of laborers is small' (LT 135; cf. Jn 4:35; Mt 9:37).

Thérèse does not hesitate to interpret the silences of the gospels. When Jesus speaks of 'things' that 'are hidden from the wise and prudent and revealed to little ones' (Mt 11:25), he does not tell us what they are. Thérèse tells us: they are 'the *things* of His *love*' (SS, p. 105). She will even change the words of Jesus himself. 'You will find rest for your souls' (Mt 11:28), he says; and Thérèse interprets: 'you will find rest for your *little* souls' (LC, p. 44). Again, Jesus gives no indication of who will 'sit at my right or at my left' in the kingdom (Mt 20:23). For Thérèse, these places are 'reserved to little children' (LC, p. 215). She recalls the priestly prayer of *John* 17 at length, skips over some verses and inverts the order of others (cf. SS, pp. 255-7). Most of all, she makes this prayer of Jesus her own: 'I dare to borrow the words You addressed to the heavenly Father' (SS, p. 254). We could also take her great discovery in reading *1Corinthians* 13: that 'the Church *had a Heart* (SS, p. 194). In fact, Paul does not here use the word 'heart'. It is Thérèse who infers it from his context. She adds to the text without betraying it.

Her superior spoke of Thérèse as of one 'whose head is filled with tricks... a *comedienne*... She can ... make you split your sides with laughter' (LC, p. 16). This sense of humour saved Thérèse from taking herself too seriously, even in her approach to the scriptures. 'It is a curious thing,' she said, 'when I open the Gospels, I nearly always come across the phrase "little children".' Then she added, tongue in cheek: 'Unless it's ... "brood of vipers"!'[16] Even on her deathbed, she read the story of the Good Samaritan with a touch of humour: 'I'm like this "half-dead" traveller,' she said: 'half-dead, half-alive' (LC, p. 174). At times, she was conscious of even shocking those around her with her daring, with her free and easy approach.

Thérèse (right) as sacristan in November 1896.

In and with the Church

Thérèse felt that she was fully in tune with the voice of the Church. She also, in the spirit of Teresa of Avila, read the scriptures as a true daughter of the Church. Likewise, Thérèse willingly submitted her insights to the scrutiny of Church representatives, as she wanted to be one in mind and heart with the community of believers in everything. When she wrote her *Act of Oblation to Merciful Love*, she asked her prioress to have it checked by a theologian. He approved everything except for one word. She had written of her 'infinite'

---

16   See *ibid.*, p. 32.

desires; he changed it to 'immense'. Thérèse accepted. Her offering had been approved – officially. She was at peace. She was living the word of God in communion with the praying Church, in the heart of the Church and at the service of the Church – the whole Church.

The 'Little Way' itself, like the scriptures, was born in response to particular needs and problems. It sprang from Thérèse's lived experience in the day-to-day struggle of faith. Like the early Christian community, Thérèse read the scriptures in the light of her own experience. Before taking up her pen to write *Story of a Soul*, she knelt in prayer at the foot of Mary's statue and 'opening the Holy Gospels,' she said, 'my eyes fell on these words: "And going up a mountain, he called to him men of his *own choosing*, and they came to him" [Mk 3:3]. This is the mystery of my vocation, my whole life' (SS, p. 13). It is scripture that would give her the key to this unfolding mystery.

Thérèse's vocation to pray for sinners developed gradually. It was confirmed at the age of fourteen and a half at the time of the Pranzini affair – a notorious criminal for whom she prayed earnestly and who repented on the scaffold. She writes: 'The cry of Jesus on the Cross sounded continually in my heart: "*I thirst!*"' (cf. Jn 19:28). Thérèse then comments: 'These words ignited within me an unknown and very living fire' (SS, p. 99). She pleaded in vain with Pope Leo XIII for permission to enter Carmel at fifteen. She later recorded her feelings: 'filled with confidence, for the Gospel of the day contained these beautiful words: "Fear not, little flock, for it is your Father's good pleasure to give you the kingdom"' (SS, p. 133; cf. Lk 12:32). Half a year later, she was a Carmelite.

Later, in Carmel, the word of God would continue to answer to her deepest needs. Totally unaware of Thérèse's troubled state of mind, the saintly Mother Geneviève reminded her of the words of Paul, '*Our God is a God of peace*' (1Cor 14:33; SS, p. 169), which diminished her anguish. Thérèse was deeply affected by her father's mental illness and in this Gethsemane experience found special meaning in the song of Isaiah's Suffering Servant, 'We esteemed him stricken, smitten by God, and afflicted' (Is 53:4).

Thérèse's greatest spiritual discovery – her legacy to the Church – began in painful questioning that only scripture could resolve. She was tormented by the problem of how a 'little' person like herself could reach the heights of sanctity. She found the solution in the words of Isaiah, '*you shall be carried at the breasts*' (Is 66:12; SS, pp. 188.208). Later, in her overriding desire to share every vocation, she read Paul's hymn to love (1Cor 13). With it, she found her true place in the Church, having discovered in that moment that this vocation would embrace all the others: 'MY VOCATION IS LOVE!' (SS, p. 194), she exclaimed.

Words of love

As Christians privileged to live in the wake of Vatican II, we are blessed with the incomparable fruits of recent biblical research. Not so Thérèse. She was not aware of the textual composition of the biblical books, the so-called literary forms, the 'synoptic question', the theories of inspiration.[17] Rarely, if ever, did she have direct access to a complete copy of the Bible.[18] Many of her favourite scripture texts were only discovered at second hand, mostly from spiritual books such as *The Imitation of Christ*, the writings of John of the Cross, or the little black leather notebook in which Céline had copied out scriptural passages before entering Carmel.[19] Today, works on the Bible can help us enormously to discover, read and assimilate the scriptures better. We should accept these admirable helps in the spirit of Thérèse: with openness, enthusiasm and gratitude. But they are of little value unless we are resolved to listen to the word of God like Thérèse: with the heart of a child, surrendered to the movements of the Spirit. The charism of Thérèse may be expressed in these words of Vatican II: 'the nourishment of the Scriptures for the people of God, thereby enlightening their minds, strengthening their wills, and setting hearts on fire with the love of God'.[20] At the top of one of her poems, Thérèse jotted down some words which our Lord addressed to Saint Gertrude. They speak reams about Thérèse's approach to the scriptures:

> My daughter, seek those words of mine which most exude love. Write them down, and then, keeping them preciously like relics, take care to reread them often. When a friend wishes to reawaken the original vigour of his affection in the heart of his friend, he tells him: 'Remember what you felt in your heart when I said such and such a word,' or 'Do you remember your feelings at such a time, on such a day, in such a place?'... Be assured then that the most precious relics of mine on earth are my words of love, the words which have come from my most sweet Heart.[21]

In this passage, we can hear again the voice of God through the prophet Hosea: 'I will speak tenderly to her heart ... she will answer as in the days of her youth'

---

17 An observation well made in T. E. Bird, 'The Use of Sacred Scripture in the "Autobiography"', *Sicut Parvuli*, vol. lxviii, no. 1, 2004, p. 29.

18 See Christopher O'Donnell, O. Carm., *Prayer: Insights from St Thérèse of Lisieux*, (Dublin: Veritas, 2001), p. 76.

19 *Ibid.*, pp. 72-3. See also the chapter by Alexander Vella in this volume.

20 *Dei Verbum* (*Dogmatic Constitution on Divine Revelation*) 23.

21 See *The Life and Revelations of Saint Gertrude*, (Westminster: Christian Classics, 1983), p. 460.

Mosaic of Thérèse overlooking the tomb of Pope Pius XI in St. Peter's Basilica, Rome.

(Hos 2:14-15). For Thérèse, the word of God comes straight from the heart of God. It is a word of love, calling for a response of love. She was to learn this lesson early on in life. She was only fourteen when she developed what she calls 'an extreme desire for learning' (SS, p. 101). Her mind expanded and her thirst for knowledge grew, she tells us. But already she had discovered that the deeper knowledge of God's word could come only through love. It was a crucial moment in her spiritual growth. God spoke to her through the prophet Ezekiel: 'Behold, you were at the age for love' (Ezk 16:8; cf. SS, p. 101).

Love must take priority. The scriptures are not just an intellectual exercise. Thérèse echoes the important lesson of the Council: 'in the sacred books, the Father who is in heaven meets His children with great love and speaks with them'.[22] She reaffirms with her life that 'the force and power in the word of God is so great that it remains the support and energy of the Church, the strength of faith for her children, the food of the soul, the pure and perennial source of spiritual life'.[23] It is the scriptures that have been canonised in the life of Thérèse.[24]

---

22 *Dei Verbum* (*Dogmatic Constitution on Divine Revelation*) 21.
23 *Ibid.* 21.
24 See Eugene McCaffrey, O.C.D., 'Thérèse of Lisieux: A Pilgrim Saint', *Mount Carmel*, vol. 50/4, 2002, p. 25, where he states: 'I love the story told by Canon Taylor, one of the first translators of her autobiography into English, about two parish priests who met on the steps of St. Peter's on May 17th, 1925, the day Thérèse was canonised. "Do you know what has happened today?" one said to the other. "Of course I do," came the reply, "a saint was canonised." "No," his friend replied, "it was the gospel itself that was canonised."'

Jesus, 'my only love'[25]

The experience of her weakness drove Thérèse to the gospels. She had a tremendous need for love. 'The Spirit of Love sets me aflame with his fire,' she says in one of her poems; 'I want to be set on fire with his Love' (PN 17, stanzas 2.15). She must find someone to love who is weak, frail and vulnerable like herself; and, like herself, passionately in need of love. She does. It is Jesus. He is the human face of God. 'The Word became flesh' (Jn 1:14), with all the weakness to which flesh is heir, except sin (Heb 4:15). Jesus sleeps through a storm – which, as we have seen, is one of Thérèse's favourite gospel scenes (Mk 4:35-41); and he stops to rest by Jacob's Well, tired and thirsty (Jn 4:4-42). She needs a God like this: weak, little, needy – quite simply, human. She can walk with this Jesus at her side, even run, for he is a companion and a friend. Jesus is her 'only Friend whom I love' (PN 23, stanza 5).

The Word truly became weakness for Thérèse. She repeats his cry, '*I thirst!*' (SS, p. 99; Jn 19:28). His 'thirst' was a thirst for love, reaching out for love when he said to the Samaritan woman, 'Give me to drink' (Jn 4:7). Thérèse says, 'it was the *love* of His poor creature the Creator of the universe was seeking. He was thirsty for love' (SS, p. 189). At the heart of the fourth gospel, Jesus cries out again for that love: 'If anyone thirsts, let that person come to me and drink' (Jn 7:37). In her poem to the Sacred Heart, the thirst of Thérèse becomes one with the thirst of the Magdalen. She does not dwell on the symbol of the pierced heart so popular in her day but lingers with the Magdalen, weeping, looking for the one she loves. Thérèse cries out:

> 'I need a heart burning with tenderness,
> Who will be my support forever,
> Who loves everything in me, even my weakness...
> And who never leaves me day or night.'...
> I must have a God who takes on my nature
> And becomes my brother and is able to suffer! (PN 23, stanza 4)

Mercy and justice meet

On the feast of the Trinity, 1895, Thérèse made her celebrated *Act of Oblation to Merciful Love* (Pri 6).[26] But right at the heart of this prayer to God's *mercy*, she also speaks of his *justice*: 'I wish...to be clothed in Your own *Justice*'. She

---

25 Thérèse engraved the words, 'Jesus is my only love!', on the lintel of her door: see Pierre Descouvemont & Helmuth Nils Loose, *Thérèse and Lisieux*, (Toronto: Novalis / Grand Rapids, MI: Eerdmans, 1996), p. 261, which also contains a photograph of it.
26 The *Act of Oblation* can also be found in SS, pp. 276-7.

writes that before making her offering, 'I was thinking about the souls who offer themselves as victims of God's Justice in order to turn away the punishments reserved to sinners, drawing them upon themselves' (SS, p. 180). The Baptist speaks of this God of justice with his words, 'Who taught you to flee from the wrath to come?' (Mt 3:7). Here we have a God of vengeance, threatening 'fire and brimstone' – a kind of heavenly Shylock exacting his pound of flesh, even the last drop of blood.

This was not the God Thérèse found reflected in the heart of Jesus. Her God proclaimed himself 'gentle and humble of heart' (Mt 11:29) – another of Thérèse's favourite gospel texts. She knew, as if by intuition, that mercy and justice, in a true biblical sense, do not necessarily exclude or contradict each other but can sit easily side by side. As we read in the *Book of Wisdom*: 'Ever should justice and mercy go hand in hand' (Wis 12:19). They are significant parallels, the one explaining the other. As the psalmist writes:

> I have not hidden your *justice* in my heart but declared your *faithful help*...
> Your *merciful love* and your *truth* will always guard me. (Ps 39:11-12)[27]

Here, we might add the words of Isaiah: 'The Lord ... exalts himself to show mercy to you. For the Lord is a God of justice' (Is 30:18). No wonder Thérèse could cry out: 'To be just is not only to exercise severity in order to punish the guilty; it is also to recognize right intentions and to reward virtue. I expect as much from God's justice as from His mercy. It is because He is just that "He is compassionate and filled with gentleness, slow to punish, and abundant in mercy, for He knows our frailty, He remembers we are only dust. As a father has tenderness for his children, so the Lord has compassion on us!!"' (LT 226; cf. Ps 102:8.14.13).

Thérèse is drawn especially by the unrequited love of God in which justice and mercy fuse. 'On every side this love is unknown, rejected,' she writes sadly. 'Is Your disdained Love going to remain closed up within Your Heart?' (SS, pp. 180-1). Her prayer of oblation ends with her own painful cry of love to God, asking him to allow 'the waves of *infinite tenderness* shut up within [him] to overflow into [her] soul' (SS, p. 277). Mercy and justice fuse for Thérèse in the 'real tenderness of His infinite Love' (SS, p. 189) – this is the heart of our God who thirsts, so often in vain, to share his love with his people.

---

27 The numbering and text of the Psalms follow the Grail version in *The Psalms: A New Translation*, (London & Glasgow: Fontana, 1963).

The weakness of God[28]

Thérèse longed to be ever more identified with the weakness of Jesus. She expressed it all in one simple aspiration: 'Make me Resemble you, Jesus!...' (Pri 11). And her prayer was certainly answered. This deep longing led her inexorably to the passion.[29] There, she was to plunge ever more deeply into the mystery of love revealed in human weakness. She recalled that as a young girl, 'The first [sermon] I *did understand* and which *touched me deeply* was a sermon on the Passion' (SS, p. 42). But she was to discover the passion again later, in a strange and entirely new way – in the face of Jesus.

At first, devotion to the Holy Face had no special appeal for Thérèse. But the discovery of it was to coincide with the mysterious mental illness of her father, who had always radiated for her the beauty of God's love. That experience now gave way to the image of her father as a man of sorrows: 'Until my coming to Carmel, I had never fathomed the depths of the treasures hidden in the Holy Face,' she said (SS, p. 152). It was, however, through the Servant Songs of Isaiah that Thérèse really entered deeply into the mystery of love hidden and revealed in human weakness: 'There was no beauty in him... no comeliness...' (Is 53:2). She confided to Pauline: 'These words of Isaias ... have made the whole foundation of my devotion to the Holy Face, or, to express it better, the foundation of all my piety' (LC, p. 135). Thérèse would continue to contemplate the love of God in her 'gentle and lowly' Saviour, his radiant face now distorted by pain, like a beautiful object reflected on rippling water. In the infirmary where Thérèse lived out her final agony, there was a fresco on the wall representing Jesus in Gethsemane. He surrenders to the pain and suffering; he accepts the sorrow and confusion, the fear and loneliness: 'Abba, Father! ... not what I will but what you will' (Mk 14:36). It is all part of the mystery of God's infinite love revealed in human weakness.

Thérèse would not in any way soften the lesson of Isaiah's words and their impact on her life. 'Let us not believe we can love without suffering, without suffering much,' she said (LT 89). Even on her deathbed, she recited phrases from the Servant Songs, making them her own: 'I desired that, like the Face of Jesus, "my face be truly hidden, that no one on earth would know me"' (SS,

---

28 See the author's *St. Thérèse: The Gospels Rediscovered*, (Darlington Carmel, [1983]), section 'The Weakness of God', pp. 53-61.

29 For an in-depth treatment of the theme of suffering in Thérèse, see André Combes, *St. Thérèse and Suffering: The Spirituality of St. Thérèse in its Essence*, (Dublin: M H Gill & Son, 1951); Christopher O'Donnell, O.Carm., *Love in the Heart of the Church: The Mission of Thérèse of Lisieux*, (Dublin: Veritas, 1997), pp. 71-98. See also the popular and practical approaches of: Vincent O'Hara, O.C.D., '"His face was as though hidden": St Thérèse's Understanding of Suffering', *Mount Carmel*, vol. 48/4, 2001, pp. 25-33; Frances Hogan, *Suffering and Prayer in the Life of St Thérèse*, (Darlington Carmel, 1988); Murchadh Ó Madagáin, *Thérèse of Lisieux: Through Love and Suffering*, (London: St Pauls, 2003).

p. 152; cf. Is 53:3); 'I, too, have desired to be without beauty, alone in treading the winepress, unknown to everyone' (LC, p. 135; cf. Is 53:2; 63:3). In Carmel, Thérèse had chosen a life of prayer and sacrifice 'hidden with Christ in God' (Col 3:3). She had embarked on a way of total self-giving in love and had found her model in the Suffering Servant – forgotten, hidden and unknown. For her, a life of sacrifice meant taking up her cross daily to follow this Jesus. It was love in action.

Thérèse expresses beautifully her desire to remove all the layers of selfishness and to be stripped of everything for love of Jesus in her simple image of 'an unpetalled rose' (PN 51). Naïve, childish, sentimental it may seem to some, even mawkish. But the reality it speaks of for Thérèse is the total and absolute self-giving of her response to love, revealed in what she calls 'the HIDDEN BEAUTIES of Jesus', the Suffering Servant (LT 108). She is never deterred by weakness in her resolve to give everything. She assures us that we do not have to suffer heroically, nor even courageously. Here again, we glimpse something of the originality of Thérèse. The worst kind of suffering, she tells us, is not being able to suffer *well* (cf. LC, p. 152) – though 'well' does not mean 'grandly'. 'What an unspeakable joy to carry our Crosses FEEBLY,' she said (LT 82). 'Let us suffer ... without courage! ... (Jesus suffered in *sadness*! Without sadness would the soul suffer! ...) And still we would like to suffer generously, grandly! ... Céline! what an illusion! ... We'd never want to fall? ... What does it matter, my Jesus, if I fall at each moment; *I see* my weakness through this and this is a great gain for me' (LT 89). Her Jesus cried out in Gethsemane; he 'sweated blood' (Lk 22:44) and 'offered up prayers and supplications, with loud cries and tears' (Heb 5:7). On his way to Calvary, he stumbled and fell – again and again and again.

Grace and truth

Thérèse was also to discover that the Word made weakness was 'full of grace and truth' (Jn 1:14). We know that she regretted not knowing the original biblical languages of Hebrew and Greek (LC, p. 132). So we can only surmise her delight, had she known that the Hebrew word for 'grace' is *hesed*[30] and that it refers to God's saving love, his *merciful* love: 'It is for love of you,' God tells his people, 'and to keep the oath he swore to your fathers that Yahweh brought you out with a mighty hand and redeemed you from the house of slavery' (Dt 7:8). It is God's covenant love, his mercy through and through. In the Old Testament, 'grace' and 'truth' are linked: 'Your merciful love and your truth will always

---

30 See section 'God's Enduring Love', in the author's *Fire of Love: Praying with Thérèse of Lisieux*, (Boston, Massachusetts: Pauline Books & Media, 2004), pp. 61-3.

*Thérèse lying ill in the cloister of the Lisieux Carmel;
this was the last photograph taken of Thérèse alive, on 30th August 1897,
exactly one month before her death.*

guard me' (Ps 39:12). The Hebrew for 'truth' is *emeth*: it refers to 'truth' as God's 'fidelity' to his covenant love, enduring in spite of the weakness of his people – their sins, their failures, their infidelities. The psalmist expresses it well: 'Indeed, how good is the Lord, eternal his merciful love. He is faithful from age to age' (Ps 99:5). *Hesed* and *emeth* express God's enduring love for his people. Paul's words capture the meaning exactly: 'We may be unfaithful, but he is always faithful for he cannot disown his own self' (2Tm 2:13; cf. Ps 116.135).

But *hesed* is also closely linked to another Hebrew term, *rahamim*, which denotes a mother's love for the child of her womb. The psalmist cries out at the marvels of this love: 'For it was you who created my being, knit me together in my mother's womb' (Ps 138:13). This love has all the feminine qualities of a caring mother's tender love – patience, understanding, always the readiness to forgive. In Jesus, Thérèse discovered the maternal heart of God, eternal and merciful love shining through human weakness, thirsting for her love. She says:

'I felt at the bottom of my heart that...God is more tender than a mother' (SS, p. 174). She expresses it beautifully in one of her poems, 'Jesus Alone':

> O you who knew how to create the mother's heart,
> I find in you the tenderest of Fathers!
> My only Love, Jesus, Eternal Word,
> For me your heart is more than maternal. (PN 36, stanza 2)

A celebration of littleness

Thérèse explains how her way to God grew out of the experience of her own weakness. She calls it a 'Little Way' – 'very straight, very short, and totally new' (SS, p. 207). When asked about it, she replied, 'It is to recognize our nothingness, to expect everything from God as a little child expects everything from its father' (LC, p. 138). In the words of the psalmist, it is to remain before God like a 'child on its mother's breast' (Ps 130:2). In *Story of a Soul* she explains it in almost identical terms: 'this road is the *surrender* of the little child who sleeps without fear in its Father's arms' (SS, p. 188).

It would be easy to heap up quotations from the gospels in support of what Thérèse calls '*my little* doctrine' (SS, p. 189). The reply of Jesus to the question of the disciples, 'Who is the greatest in the kingdom of Heaven?' (Mt 18:1), readily comes to mind: 'In truth I tell you, unless you change and become like little children you will never enter the kingdom of Heaven. And so, those who make themselves as little as this little child are the greatest in the kingdom of Heaven' (Mt 18:3-4).[31] In *Story of a Soul*, Thérèse develops at length the further implications of her gospel teaching on spiritual childhood. We find it in the record of her last retreat (SS, pp. 187-200) – just a few brief pages of incredible spiritual depth.[32] These are not simply a collection of beautiful thoughts, nor are they mere speculation or theory. They are a faith-filled interpretation, illumined by scripture, of her personal experience of living out her 'Little Way'. Love, trust, surrender, confidence and her vast desires are here linked, and have to be linked, with littleness. For Thérèse, greatness in the gospel sense is inseparable from the weakness of a child.

---

31 Although there are several gospel passages on spiritual childhood which Thérèse does not quote in her writings, we know from the testimony of others how familiar she was with these texts: see *La Bible, op. cit.*, pp. 192-3; LC, p. 213.

32 This central section of *Story of a Soul* is also known as 'Manuscript B'. See below, section 'A "Little Way" of vast desires', for a treatment of Thérèse's discovery of 'love in the heart of the Church'. Conrad De Meester, O.C.D., examines this turning-point in Thérèse's life: see his *The Power of Confidence: Genesis and Structure of the 'Way of Spiritual Childhood' of Saint Thérèse of Lisieux*, (New York: Alba House, 1998), pp. 183-208.

Part of the 'Little Way' – an integral aspect, though still only a part – is about doing little things for God and doing them well. Again and again, Thérèse insists on this. 'Jesus does not demand great actions from us,' she writes, 'but simply *surrender* and *gratitude* ... He has no need of our works but only of our *love... love* is proved by works... Jesus, I am too little to perform great actions ... I am a *very little soul* and ... I can offer God only *very little things*' (SS, pp. 188.189.196.200.250). Echoing John of the Cross, she says: '*the smallest act of* PURE LOVE *is of more value to [the Church] than all other works together*' (SS, p. 197; cf. SC 29:2). Thérèse's 'nothings' will please Jesus (SS, p. 197). She will prove her love to him, she says, by 'not allowing one little sacrifice to escape, not one look, one word, profiting by all the smallest things and doing them through love' (SS, p. 196). It is God's love that makes these tiniest actions 'infinitely valuable' (SS, p. 197) and pleasing to God.

But doing little things for God is all part of acknowledging and accepting our own littleness and weakness. This, she confesses repeatedly, is essential for all who wish to follow her 'Little Way': 'Is there a soul more *little*, more powerless than mine?' she asks (SS, p. 193); 'I am the smallest of creatures; I know my misery and my feebleness' (SS, p. 195). All these facets of Thérèse's teaching are summed up briefly in one sentence: 'I feel that if You found a soul weaker and littler than mine...You would be pleased to grant it still greater favors, provided it abandoned itself with total confidence to Your Infinite Mercy' (SS, p. 200). Yet, for all her 'extreme littleness' (SS, p. 198), Thérèse experiences 'great aspirations' (SS, p. 197), 'measureless desires' (SS, p. 197), '*infinite desires*' (LT 107) – 'desires and longings which reach even unto infinity' (SS, p. 193). She was confused by this and asked the question: 'O Jesus, my Love, my Life, how can I combine these contrasts? How can I realize the desires of my poor *little soul*?' (SS, p. 192). Her 'Little Way' is not a contradiction of the greatness of her desires: it is precisely the 'Little Way' that can provide the explanation.

A 'Little Way' of vast desires

The remarkable thing about the 'Little Way' is that these vast desires of Thérèse spring from the experience of her own powerlessness and weakness. In fact, the deeper she plunged into the abyss of her own littleness, the greater and more intense her desires became. At an early age, Thérèse already felt that she was destined for '*glory*' – the glory of 'becoming a great *saint*' (SS, p. 72). One incident speaks volumes. 'Father,' she once said to a visiting priest, 'I want to become a saint, I want to love the Good God as much as St Teresa.' 'What pride and what presumption!' he replied. 'Moderate your rash desires.' Undaunted, she insisted, 'But, Father, I do not regard these as rash desires, I can truly aspire to sanctity, even to a more exalted sanctity, if I wish, than that of St Teresa, for Our Lord said, "Be perfect as your heavenly Father is perfect." You can see, Father, how vast the field is; and it seems to me that I have the right to run in it.'[33] But by the time she came to describe her 'Little Way', her desires were virtually limitless, infinite. Technically, we might call this an experience of self-transcendence. She found that there was a longing in her that went beyond every boundary, breaking open every goal. It was a need, a hunger, a thirst to embrace every vocation in the Church, including that of the priest, apostle, doctor, martyr – in short, to be 'everything' (SS, pp. 192.194).

Again, it was the scriptures that provided an answer to the 'veritable martyrdom' (SS, p. 193) which her unsatisfied desires were causing her. 'I opened the Epistles of St. Paul,' she tells us, 'to find some kind of answer' (SS, p. 193). In vain, she sought for her place among the different members of the Church listed by Paul (1Cor 12). Then he goes on to speak of the 'way' of love (1Cor 13). We can only marvel at Thérèse's astounding and original development of the apostle's teaching on love. Paul never mentions the 'heart' among the members of the Church. But Thérèse does: 'I understood that the Church *had a Heart*,' she exclaims, '*and that this Heart was BURNING WITH LOVE*... I understood that LOVE COMPRISED ALL VOCATIONS...THAT IT WAS ETERNAL!... MY VOCATION IS LOVE!... in the heart of the Church, my Mother, I shall be *Love*. Thus I shall be everything' (SS, p. 194). Yes, love is eternal, infinite – like her own infinite desires. But Thérèse reminds us explicitly that it was through entering deeply into her own weakness and littleness that she attained all her desires: 'I, abasing myself to the very depths of my nothingness, raised myself so high that I was able to attain my end' (SS, p. 194).[34] And she repeats this lesson in no uncertain terms: 'because of my weakness,' she cries out, 'it has pleased You, O Lord, to grant my *little childish desires* and You desire, today, to grant other desires that are *greater* than the universe' (SS, p. 193).

Capacity for the infinite

The human heart can go to the lengths of God; it is 'capable of God'.[35] The theologian who changed Thérèse's expression in her *Act of Oblation* from

33 See *La Bible, op. cit.*, p. 158; also, Guy Gaucher, O.C.D., *The Spiritual Journey of St Thérèse of Lisieux*, (London: Darton, Longman & Todd), 1987, p. 107. The visiting priest was Fr. Blino, S.J.

34 These words are an allusion to the poem of John of the Cross, '*I went out seeking love...*': *The Collected Works of Saint John of the Cross*, trans. Kieran Kavanaugh, O.C.D. & Otilio Rodriguez, O.C.D., (Washington, D.C.: I.C.S. Publications, 1991), Poem 6.

35 Thomas Aquinas, commenting on the writings of Augustine, describes the human person as *capax Dei* ('capable of God' or 'fit to receive God'): see *Summa Theologica* I-II q. 113 a. 10; cf. Augustine, *De Trinitate* 1.14 c. 8. See, too, *Catechism of the Catholic Church*, section 'Man's Capacity for God', 27-43. Augustine

'infinite desires' to 'immense desires' missed the full import of her experience.[36] She wrote 'infinite', she repeated it elsewhere (LT 107; cf. SS, p. 192), and she meant it. In fact, the nature of desire is determined not by the person who desires, but by the object of longing. John of the Cross speaks of the 'deep caverns' of the human spirit – its faculties of memory, intellect and will: 'They are as deep as the boundless goods of which they are capable,' he explains, 'since anything less than the infinite fails to fill them' (*The Living Flame of Love* 3:18). He continues: 'capable of infinite goods ... they cannot receive these infinite goods until they are completely empty' (LF 3:18). Augustine repeats the same lesson: 'This is our life, to be exercised by desire. But we are exercised by holy desire only in so far as we have cut off our longings from the love of the world ... empty that which is to be filled.'[37]

It was precisely this emptying out of herself, entering into the profound depths of her own weakness or nothingness, that put Thérèse in touch with her vast desires, her sheer emptiness and capacity for God, for the infinite. She draws on her own original interpretation of a rather strange gospel text in support of her experience. It is the conclusion to the parable of the unjust steward (Lk 16:1-9): 'Make use of the riches which render one unjust in order to make friends who will receive you into everlasting dwellings' (Lk 16:9). For Thérèse, these 'riches' are '*my desires of being everything*' (SS, p. 195). It is these that will open to her the kingdom of heaven. But they need not necessarily do so. The wealth of her desires can be misdirected to something other than God. The psalmist laments these disordered appetites that restrict the human spirit: 'how long will your hearts be closed, will you love what is futile and seek what is false?' (Ps 4:3). Thérèse saw clearly that misguided desires 'were the riches that would be able to render me unjust' (SS, p. 195). Any such inordinate and self-centred desire would savour of yielding to the primeval temptation, 'You will be like God' (Gn 3:5), stifling our deepest need of God by gratifying our selfish desires with something less than him.

In describing her own desire for littleness, Thérèse may give the impression, at times, that she is proud of her own weakness: 'I am simply resigned to see myself always imperfect and in this I find my joy... It seems to me I'm humble...' (SS, p. 158; LC, p. 205). But even if she appears to be boasting, she is in fact

---

also writes: 'by delaying the fulfilment of desire God stretches it, by making us desire he expands the soul, and by this expansion he increases its capacity': from his treatise on the *First Letter of St John*, in *Divine Office*, vol. I, p. 538.

36   Although 'immense' literally means 'measureless' or 'without measure or limit' and so may rightly be used as a synonym for 'infinite' – as John of the Cross himself uses it: *inmensos ... infinitos bienes* (*The Living Flame of Love* 3:18) – the effect of the theologian's change was to lessen the impact of Thérèse's 'infinite' desires.

37   From the treatise of Saint Augustine on the *First Letter of St. John*, in *Divine Office*, vol. I, p. 538. See also, on desire as exercised in prayer, his letter to Proba, in *Divine Office*, vol. III, pp. 661-2.

speaking the language of Paul who 'glories in [his] weakness' (2Cor 12:9) so as to experience the strength of Christ: 'it is in my weakness that I glory,' writes Thérèse, 'and I expect each day to discover new imperfections in myself' (SS, p. 224). And she does not hesitate to link the greatest grace of her life to the discovery of her own weakness: 'I prefer to agree very simply that the Almighty has done great things in [me] ... and the greatest thing is to have shown [me my] *littleness*, [my] impotence' (SS, p. 210). 'I feel that if You found a soul weaker and littler than mine,' she says to Jesus, and then adds, 'which is impossible' (SS, p. 200). Is this false modesty or lack of humility, her claiming to be littler than anyone else could ever be? Quite the contrary: it confirms that Thérèse is in touch with her own infinite emptiness for God. Nobody can be smaller than one who is immeasurably small. In this sense, nobody can be more little than anyone else. Thérèse has recognised that she is limitlessly small, immeasurably empty for God. How much littler can anyone possibly be than Thérèse in the immensity of her sheer desire for God?

Infinite emptiness

In his discussion of the human faculties, or 'caverns', John of the Cross explains: 'when these caverns are empty and pure, the thirst, hunger, and yearning of the spiritual feeling is intolerable' (LF 3:18). Thérèse, likewise, speaks of her desires as 'a veritable martyrdom' (SS, p. 193).[38] In her language, this emptiness is her littleness and weakness and neediness – the radical poverty of her total capacity for God. Her heart, in John's words, is 'emptied, purged and cleansed of every affection for creatures' (LF 3:18) – infinitely little and totally empty for God. Limitlessly little, Thérèse experiences the *vast emptiness* of her boundless capacity for the infinite. John of the Cross explains: 'The capacity of these caverns is deep because the object of this capacity, namely God, is profound and infinite. Thus in a certain fashion their capacity is infinite, and their languishing and suffering are infinite death' (LF 3:22).

Entering into the abyss of her own littleness, weakness and powerlessness, Thérèse experienced her total capacity for God released in the vast hunger and yearning of her painful desires which only an infinite God of love could activate and fully satisfy. Her limitless capacity was at full stretch, her restless heart in the pain of separation but not yet completely at rest in God. Thérèse experienced herself as an immense and limitless capacity for God, and it was precisely her unsatisfied desires that impelled her forward in absolute confidence and trust

---

38 See also Teresa's treatment of anxious and painful desires: *The Interior Castle* VI:11:2.5, in *The Collected Works of St. Teresa of Avila*, trans. Kieran Kavanaugh, O.C.D. & Otilio Rodriguez, O.C.D., Volume 2, (Washington, D.C.: I.C.S. Publications, 1980).

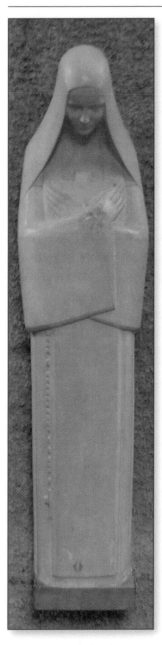

A statue of Thérèse in the chapel dedicated to her in the Basilica of St. Pius X in Lourdes.

towards the promised gift of God himself: 'Not that I have secured it already,' she could have said with Paul, 'nor reached my goal, but I am still running trying to capture the prize for which Christ Jesus captured me... I do not reckon myself as having taken hold of it; I can only say that forgetting all that lies behind me, and straining forward to what lies in front, I am racing towards the finishing-point to win the prize of God's heavenly call in Christ Jesus' (Ph 3:12-14).

At first, Thérèse seemed troubled by her vast desires. But all that changed as they became highly important for her in defining her 'Little Way'. They gave meaning to her experience of endless need, the transcendent aspect of what it means to be made for God – fully human in her endless desire, and in her openness to be touched by God's love in her sheer nothingness. These desires are not unreasonable, even though they reach beyond reason: to a self-transcendence that is sublime. Thérèse's 'Little Way' is, in fact, a perfect way to be fully human. The challenge of it is to recognise this and to live it fully in total confidence, relying unreservedly on God's merciful love. To do this requires a trust as infinite as desire – again, reasonable beyond reason: 'my own folly is this: to trust,' writes Thérèse (SS, p. 200). This requires especially a radical self-emptying, like the self-emptying of God himself in his Son – the divine *kenosis* in the Word made flesh (Ph 2:7). 'I have found the secret of possessing Your flame,' Thérèse says. 'Yes, in order that Love be fully satisfied, it is necessary that It lower Itself... to nothingness and transform this nothingness into *fire*' (SS, p. 195). For love to be love in God, it needs to give itself away, empty itself; for love to be love in Thérèse, it needed to do the same: empty itself, give itself away.[39] So, in the 'Little Way' of

---

39 Cf. the definition of God's love by Edith Stein – 'God is love, and love is goodness giving itself away' – in *The Hidden Life*, trans. Waltraut Stein, (Washington, D.C.: I.C.S. Publications, 1992), p. 38.

self-emptying surrender to God's merciful love, the heights and the depths are one.

Discovering love

For all her great desires, the spirituality of Thérèse is deeply embedded in the daily demands of community living. Keenly aware of her own weakness, she found in the new commandment[40] the key to the mystery of that same human frailty in others. Near the end of her life, Thérèse wrote of love: 'God has given me the grace to understand what charity is; I understood it before, it is true, but in an imperfect way... I applied myself especially to *loving God*, and it is in loving Him that I understood my love was not to be expressed only in words' (SS, p. 219). All her life, she had walked the way of God's commandment of love, never refusing him anything since the age of three (cf. SS, p. 279). But it was only in loving him that she discovered the deeper mysteries of that love. This discovery was God's gift to her – his gift in response to her love: 'those who love me will be loved by my Father, and I will love them and reveal myself to them' (Jn 14:21).

As always, Thérèse focuses on Jesus. He is the exemplar. He points to Calvary and says: 'Love one another as I have loved you' (Jn 15:12; 13:34). 'How,' Thérèse asks, 'did Jesus love His disciples and why did He love them?' (SS, p. 220). She replies: 'it was not their natural qualities that could have attracted Him... they were poor ignorant fishermen filled with earthly thoughts. And still Jesus called them *his friends, his brothers*' (SS, p. 220). In using the word 'friends', she is here borrowing from *John*: 'I have called you friends' (Jn 15:5). Jesus does not love his disciples *because* they are his 'friends'; rather, they are his friends because he *first loved them*: 'In this is love, not that we loved God but that he loved us... We love, because he first loved us' (1 Jn 4:10, 19). The thought-pattern of Thérèse is often the same as that of the fourth evangelist, and her words echo clearly the teaching of his gospel. She writes: 'He desires to see [His disciples] reign with Him in the kingdom of His Father, and to open that kingdom to them He wills to die on the cross, for He said: "*Greater love than this no man has than that he lay down his life for his friends*"' (SS, p. 220; Jn 15:13; cf. 13:34). There, on Calvary, Thérèse finds the full and complete revelation of Jesus' pure and selfless love – redemptive and sacrificial. And so, she can say, 'I am prepared to lay down my life for [my Sisters]' (SS, p. 239).

---

40   See note 43 below for the section 'An impossible commandment?'.

Love's stark realism

Thérèse with Our Lady of Mount Carmel and the Infant Jesus; window at Whitefriar Street Carmelite Church, Dublin.

'*Illusions*,' said Thérèse, 'God gave me the grace *not to have* A SINGLE ONE when entering Carmel. I found the religious life to be *exactly* as I had imagined it, no sacrifice astonished me' (SS, p. 149). With a clear, keen eye sharpened by her own struggle to love others and by her observations of community living, Thérèse discovered 'that all souls have very much the same struggles to fight' (SS, p. 239) and lays bare for us, in the final part of *Story of a Soul*, the full demands of fraternal love.[41] Yet, for all her realism, she touches human weakness with deep sympathy, understanding and warmth. Like Jesus, she 'could tell what someone had within' (Jn 2:25): the challenges, the temptations and the difficulties.

For Thérèse, every sacrifice demanded by human relationships was a real death to self. The little grains of self-love, self-complacency, self-pity, self-assertiveness provided so many occasions of self-mastery: not to insist that an object borrowed be returned because this 'would satisfy self-love' (SS, p. 229); a smile for the ungracious 'when I was tempted to answer her back in a disagreeable manner' (SS, p. 223); resisting 'a great desire to turn my head and stare at the culprit' who was irritating her (SS, p. 249), or a temptation in the laundry 'to draw back and wipe [her] face to show the Sister who was sprinkling [her]' (SS, p. 250); a kindly service done to one with 'poor crippled hands... because I knew it was not easy to please [her]' (SS, pp. 248.247); seeking out at recreation 'the least agreeable to me in order to carry out with regard to these wounded souls the office of the good Samaritan', knowing that a 'word, an amiable smile, often suffice to make a sad soul bloom' (SS, p. 246); running away 'like a deserter whenever my struggles became too violent' (SS, p. 223); when disturbed, taking 'care to appear happy and especially *to be so*' (SS, p. 228); not insisting on her rights when 'my heart was beating' with indignation (SS, p. 224).

At first glance, her language might sometimes appear exaggerated. But Thérèse was keenly sensitive and so, too, the struggle was all the more intense.

---

41 This is the third section of *Story of a Soul*, often referred to as 'Manuscript C', and written right at the end of her life.

When, for example, an article for her work is removed, 'patience is very close to abandoning me and I must take my courage in both hands in order to reclaim the missing object without bitterness' (SS, p. 226); refusing in 'such a delightful way ... what cannot be given that the refusal gives as much pleasure as the gift itself' (SS, p. 228). She exclaims, 'Ah! how contrary are the teachings of Jesus to the feelings of nature!' (SS, p. 229) and sums up everything so well: 'Ah! I understand now that charity consists in bearing with the faults of others, in not being surprised at their weakness, in being edified by the smallest acts of virtue we see them practice. But I understood above all that charity must not remain hidden in the bottom of the heart' (SS, p. 220).

The utter candour of her self-analysis and the frank confession of her struggle holds up the mirror to the stark reality and truth of the demands of community living and its essential core of sacrifice. But her humanity and sympathy for others never deserted her. She experienced the truth of John's words: 'We know that we have passed out of death into life, because we love the brethren. Whoever does not love remains in death' (1 Jn 3:14-15). The fruits of victory in her conflicts, Thérèse tells us, were peace and joy as an abiding possession: 'Ah! what peace floods the soul when she rises above natural feelings' (SS, p. 226).

Love in action

'Bear one another's burdens and so you shall fulfil the law of Christ', writes Paul (Gal 6:2). And Thérèse: 'it isn't enough to love; we must prove it' (SS, p. 225). For her, the words of scripture were not a mere repertoire of beautiful thoughts and sentiments – a mirror to look into, only to forget later what manner of person one is (cf. Jas 1:23-24). Thérèse was 'a doer of the word' and not a hearer only, deceiving herself (cf. Jas 1:22). She reiterates the lesson of Teresa of Avila, 'good works, good works' (*Interior Castle* VII:4:6): 'The most beautiful thoughts are nothing,' Thérèse tells us, 'without good works' (SS, p. 234). She recalled this when she felt challenged to put it into practice – practical Christianity! 'Not wishing to give in to the natural antipathy I was experiencing,' she writes, 'I told myself that charity must not consist in feelings but in works... I understood my love was not to be expressed only in words' (SS, pp. 222.219). Again, her thinking is along the mind of John: 'Little children, let us not love in word or speech, but in deed and in truth' (1 Jn 3:18).

Thérèse illustrates the dynamism of her love with a beautiful example which goes straight to the heart of community living. A sister in her community was displeasing to her in every way. But, as Thérèse had reminded herself that charity consists not in feelings but in works (SS, p. 222), 'I set myself to doing for this Sister,' she said, 'what I would do for the person I loved the most' (SS, p. 222). This was love in action. But even more important is the lesson of Thérèse on the true vision of faith that made this possible: 'what attracted me,' she confesses, 'was Jesus hidden in the depths of her soul' (SS, p. 223). Thérèse did not see just another sister – weak, frail, imperfect like herself. She responded to her with love and discovered Jesus in her. Or rather, it was Jesus 'hidden' in brokenness who revealed himself to Thérèse in response to her love. She experienced the truth of Matthew's gospel: 'I was hungry... thirsty... a stranger... You did it to me' (Mt 25:35-40). Beneath the surface in every human person lies the hidden beauty of God's presence waiting to be discovered.

Thérèse with Christ and his mother Mary sculpted in wood at Whitefriars, Faversham, England.

Jesus says, in the gospel of John: 'I am the vine and you are the branches' (Jn 15:5). Every word is significant for community living. Jesus is the vine – the stock and the branches – that is, the whole community. He lives on in the whole community, just as every person lives in him (cf. Jn 15:4). He works his own masterpiece in each person differently, so that everyone reflects in a unique way the face of Jesus.[42] Thérèse resonates to this teaching on Jesus as the vine: 'when especially the devil tries to place before the eyes of [her] soul the faults of such and such a Sister' (SS, p. 221), she looks deeper to the truth beneath the surface and into the hidden beauty of that person. She looks with the eyes of faith and sees Christ working there. Thérèse does not linger on the faults, failings or limitations of another sister: 'I hasten,' she says, 'to

42 Thérèse remembered well what a priest had once taught her: *'There are really more differences among souls than there are among faces'* (SS, pp. 239-40).

search out her virtues, her good intentions' – that is, Jesus at work in her sister. With startling insight, Thérèse comments: 'what appears to me as a fault can very easily be an act of virtue because of her intention' (SS, p. 221). Again, her thoughts run on the lines of John, even without explicit reference: 'Do not judge by appearances... you judge according to the flesh' (Jn 7:24; 8:15) – by human, natural standards. 'In order that this judgment be favorable,' writes Thérèse, 'or rather that I be not judged at all, I want to be charitable in my thoughts toward others at all times, for Jesus has said: *"Judge not, and you shall not be judged"'* (SS, p. 222).

An impossible commandment?[43]

Thérèse is aware of the exalted and radical demands of fraternal love: 'Love one another as I have loved you' (Jn 15:12; 13:34). So she asks the question: is this love possible? In one of the deepest and loveliest passages she ever penned, Thérèse discovers the truth of Jesus' teaching in *John*: 'Ah! Lord,' she exclaims, 'I know you don't command the impossible' (SS, p. 221). She is still aware of her weakness and imperfection. She is always conscious of that illusive 'beam' in her own eye. 'You know very well,' she writes, 'that never would I be able to love my Sisters as You love them'; then comes the solution: 'unless *You*, O my Jesus, *loved them in me*. It is because You wanted to give me this grace that You made Your *new* commandment... it gives me the assurance that Your Will is *to love in me* all those You command me to love!' (SS, p. 221). Ever practical, Thérèse goes on to draw out the implications of her teaching: 'it is Jesus alone who is acting in me, and the more united I am to Him, the more also do I love my Sisters' (SS, p. 221). That is how real community grows. We can so easily miss the reality beneath the surface, a truth open only to the eyes of faith: 'Abide in me... abide in my love' (Jn 15:4-7.9-10).

Few have ever lived the new commandment as fully as Thérèse. Her final word speaks of God's vast plan of salvation and of her – and our – place in it, as channels of his love. Again, it is scripture that helps her to express her thoughts: '*therefore have I raised you, that I may show* MY POWER *in you, and my name may be spoken of throughout all the earth*' (SS, p. 234; Ex 9:16). She goes on to explain: 'Century has followed on century since the Most High has spoken those words, and since then His conduct has undergone no change, for He is always using His creatures as instruments to carry on His work in souls'

---

43 See the author's *St Thérèse, op. cit.*, section 'An Impossible Commandment', pp. 43-52; also his 'Saint Thérèse and the New Commandment', in Thomas M. Curran, O.C.D., (ed.), *The Mind of Saint Thérèse of Lisieux*, (Dublin: Carmelite Centre of Spirituality / Bury, Greater Manchester: Koinonia, 1977), Ch. 3, pp. 26-36.

(SS, pp. 234-5). *All* believers have a mission – God's mission – as channels of his love. Yes, we are Christ, who is present, spread out everywhere, until the end of time. Like Thérèse, we are Christ's love let loose in the world.

The prayer of a child

Thérèse admits to another form of weakness: the difficulties of prayer, which is an experience common to all who try to pray. This is what makes her teaching so engaging and compelling. She herself was no stranger to distractions, the inability to concentrate, unanswered requests, aridity, loss of fervour, emptiness, and the apparent absence of God. She often slept during prayer. At times, we have all suffered such disappointments and frustrations. We, too, know what it is to struggle as she did. But for Thérèse, weakness is not an obstacle to communion with God: it is a stepping-stone to closer intimacy with him. With characteristic originality, she writes, 'I learned very quickly ... that the more one advances, the more one sees the goal is still far off. And now I am simply resigned to see myself always imperfect and in this I find my joy' (SS, p. 158).

Thérèse has lessons for all of us on how to deal with our difficulties and struggles in prayer: 'I do not have the courage to force myself to search out *beautiful* prayers in books... it really gives me a headache!' (SS, p. 242). So, what does she do? Powerless and weak like a little child, she relates to God exactly as a child: 'I do like children who do not know how to read, I say very simply to God what I wish to say, without composing beautiful sentences, and He always understands me' (SS, p. 242). In her weakness, Thérèse prays like a child who dares to say, 'Father'. This was how Jesus himself prayed at his moment of greatest desolation in Gethsemane: 'Abba, Father!' (Mk 14:36). It is also the way the early Christian community prayed: 'When we cry, "Abba, Father!" it is the Spirit himself bearing witness with our spirit that we are children of God' (Rm 8:15-16). This prayer is possible, Paul explains, because 'God has sent the Spirit of his Son into our hearts, crying, "Abba, Father!"' (Gal 4:6). Thérèse echoes his teaching: 'we cannot, without the Spirit of Love, give the name of "*Father*" to our Father in heaven' (SS, p. 234). She teaches us to pray like Jesus: a child communing in love with its Father. Whenever we, like Thérèse, 'do not know how to pray as we ought, it is the same Spirit who helps us,' says Paul, 'in our weakness' (Rm 8:26).

When Thérèse speaks of her powerlessness to pray, she confesses to sometimes finding it 'impossible to draw forth [from prayer] one single thought to unite me with God' (SS, p. 243). In the spirit of Teresa, she teaches us by her own example to resort to vocal prayer: 'I *very slowly* recite an "Our Father",' she says, 'and then the angelic salutation... they nourish my soul much more than if I had recited them precipitately a hundred times' (SS, p. 243).[44] As Teresa herself had discovered (cf. *The Way of Perfection* 30:7), so Thérèse, too, found that the Our Father could lead into deep prayer and contemplation. One day, her sister found Thérèse alone in her room, 'lost in profound contemplation'. Céline asked what she was thinking about, and Thérèse replied with tears in her eyes what a wonderful thing it was 'to call God our Father'; she was, Thérèse explained, 'meditating on the *Our Father*'.[45] Her heart had gone out to him – in an endless, aching hunger. There is a pain beyond all telling, hidden in the heart of love. It is there also in the heart of prayer – a thirst, and a longing unsatisfied. It is an aspiration of the heart, a reaching out in love.

'An aspiration of the heart'

Thérèse's teaching on prayer is embedded not just in the experience of her own weakness. It is also inseparably linked with her great desires. She describes prayer briefly, in these striking terms:

> For me, *prayer* is an aspiration of the heart, it is a simple glance directed to heaven, it is a cry of gratitude and love in the midst of trial as well as joy; finally, it is something great, supernatural, which expands my soul and unites me to Jesus. (SS, p. 242)[46]

An aspiration of the heart! 'To aspire' means, literally, 'to breathe' (*spirare*) 'towards' (*ad*) – to long, or to sigh, for *something* or *someone*. In a word, it is a desire. When the object is God, it is an outburst of love – a fling of the heart to the heart of God.

Thérèse recalls fishing expeditions with her father in the countryside. She would sit there on a river bank bedecked with flowers: 'my thoughts became very profound,' she said. 'Without knowing what it was to meditate, my soul was absorbed in real prayer. I listened to distant sounds, the murmuring of the wind... Earth then seemed to be a place of exile and I could dream only of heaven' (SS, p. 37). That was her prayer – her aspiration: her pilgrim soul in exile, longing for heaven. But Thérèse never longed for heaven alone. Her deepest longing was for Jesus. As she later wrote, again speaking of her desire for heaven:

---

44 See James McCaffrey, O.C.D., *Captive Flames: A Biblical Reading of the Carmelite Saints*, (Dublin: Veritas, 2005), Ch. 1, section 'Praying with words', p. 44.

45 See Sister Geneviève of the Holy Face (Céline Martin), *My Sister St. Thérèse*, (Rockford, Illinois: Tan Books, 1997), p. 109.

46 The first half of this passage of Thérèse has been used in the 1992 *Catechism of the Catholic Church* as the opening definition of prayer (§2558).

I think that the Heart of my Spouse is mine alone, just as mine is His alone, and I speak to Him then in the solitude of this delightful heart to heart, while waiting to contemplate Him one day face to face... (LT 122)

In these few words, we find an emphasis on the heart of God, which is integral to Carmelite prayer. When Thérèse expresses her need for solitude, she says: 'I want to hide myself for you, O Jesus! / Lovers must have solitude, / A heart-to-heart lasting night and day' (PN 17, stanza 3). Her need for withdrawal to pray means, in the words of Teresa, 'taking time frequently to be alone with [God]' (*Life* 8:5). For both Teresa and Thérèse, the essence of prayer lies in a communion or exchange of love: for Teresa, an 'intimate sharing between friends' (*Life* 8:5); for Thérèse, a 'heart-to-heart'. In her *Act of Oblation to Merciful Love*, Thérèse expands on her understanding of prayer as love. She implores God: 'look upon me only in the Face of Jesus and in His heart burning with *Love*' (SS, p. 276).

This prayer of oblation is like an extended litany of love's passionate longings. Her pleadings, 'I desire... I want... I long... I wish...', ring out the variations on her ardent need to love.

It is desire that accepts every pain: 'let us love Him enough to suffer for Him all that He wills, even spiritual pains, aridities, anxieties,' she exhorted her sister Céline and added, 'That is love pushed to the point of heroism' (LT 94). Years later, her deathbed conversation with this same sister illustrates how well Thérèse practised what she preached. 'What are you doing?' Céline asked her, finding her awake in the middle of the night. 'You should try to sleep.' 'I can't

Window at the Curia of the Carmelite Order in Rome depicting Saint Thérèse 'showering roses'.

sleep,' replied Thérèse, 'I'm suffering too much, so I am praying.' 'And what are you saying to Jesus?' 'I say nothing to Him, I love Him!' (LC, p. 228). Such was her prayer: one long, ceaseless aspiration of love in her weakness and in her pain – while, in her own phrase, 'waiting to contemplate Him one day face to face' (LT 122). She was, in the spirit of the Carmelite *Rule*, 'watching in prayer' (Chapter 10) – a woman of prayer, right to the end.

Pondering the word

Thérèse also prayed – again in the spirit of her *Rule* – by 'pondering the Lord's law day and night' (Chapter 10). Her prayer time seems to have been mainly a prolonged meditation on the gospel, listening to it prayerfully in response to the action of the Holy Spirit – even if Thérèse rarely mentions the Spirit explicitly. 'This is…what Jesus has done in my soul during my retreat,' she says: he told her to 'descend' like Zacchaeus. She then comments at length on the way of *descending*: into a place of poverty where we may 'serve as an abode for Jesus' (LT 137).[47] On another occasion, she retired in silence to her room and reflected on what Jesus thought of her many failings: 'I recalled these words He addressed one day to the adulterous woman: "Has no one condemned you?" And I, tears in my eyes, answered Him: "No one, Lord"' (LT 230; cf. Jn 8:10-11).

The life of Thérèse, like that of Mary, was one of treasuring God's word in her heart (cf. Lk 2:51; cf. 2:19), open to the Spirit. 'The Holy Spirit … will bring back to your memory everything I have said to you,' Jesus remarked (Jn 14:26). The Spirit will often 'recall' a word of scripture for Thérèse.[48] She repeats it and lets it seep into her mind and heart: 'I repeated constantly to myself these words of St. Paul: "It is no longer I that live, it is Jesus who lives in me!"' (SS, p. 79; cf. Ga 2:20). Her method of 'repetition' is as old as the *lectio divina* of the Desert Fathers and the monastic tradition. 'I repeated over and over the words of love burning in my heart,' she writes (SS, p. 103). As sacristan, she often *recalls* these words: 'You are to be holy, you who carry the vessels of the Lord' (SS, p. 172: cf. Is 52:11).

The words of scripture just came to her memory as she tried to explain God's mercy to one of the sisters. This nun later said of Thérèse: 'I was amazed that this sister, who was so young, knew so well how to show me the mercy of God, quoting passages of the psalms for me as easily as if she had read them in a

---

47 Cf. Elizabeth of the Trinity, *Heaven in Faith* 7 and *Last Retreat* 42, in *Complete Works of Elizabeth of the Trinity*, volume 1, trans. Aletheia Kane, O.C.D., (Washington, D.C.: I.C.S. Publications, 1984).

48 On the 'recalling' action of the Holy Spirit who brings the word of God back to our memory, see the author's *The Carmelite Charism: Exploring the Biblical Roots*, (Dublin: Veritas, 2004), pp. 18-20.

book'.[49] It *was* a book: the book of Jesus' own words communicated to her directly. As Thérèse once wrote:

> Jesus has no need of books or teachers to instruct souls; He teaches without the noise of words. Never have I heard Him speak, but I feel that He is within me at each moment; He is guiding and inspiring me with what I must say and do... I have frequently noticed that Jesus doesn't want me to lay up *provisions*; He nourishes me at each moment with a totally new food; I find it within me without my knowing how it is there. I believe it is Jesus Himself hidden in the depths of my poor little heart: He is giving me the grace of acting within me, making me think of all He desires me to do at the present moment. (SS, pp. 179.165)

But the Spirit does not just 'recall' the word of God in a general way. He makes it actual and relevant to the individual person. He shows Thérèse how it is realised in herself and in others: 'I ... see the words of Psalm 22 realized in me,' she said: '"The Lord is my Shepherd, I shall not want..."' (SS, p. 15; cf. Ps 22:1). She says of herself and of her companion: 'in us was realized this passage from Scripture: *A brother who is helped by a brother is like a strong city*"' (SS, p. 236; cf. Pr 18:19). Through the Spirit, Thérèse discovered, too, the significance of the word of God for the here and now, the concrete circumstances of her daily living. In keeping with a custom in the Carmel at that time, she often opened the Bible at random,[50] receiving the word that God chose to give her at that precise moment. It was a word of life for herself personally, and also for others.

Soon after entering Carmel, she wrote to her sister Céline: 'I read this morning a passage of the Gospel where it says: "I have not come to bring peace but the sword"' (LT 57; cf. Mt 10:34); this strengthened her for the trials that lay ahead. Céline also once wrote to her with a problem and Thérèse replied, 'After having read your letter, I went to prayer, and taking the gospel, I asked Jesus to find a passage for you, and this is what I found: "Behold the fig tree ..." I closed the book, I had read enough' (LT 143; cf. Lk 21:29). A year before her death, Thérèse was still meditating, pondering, praying the word of God: 'This evening, during my prayer, I meditated on some passages from Isaias which appeared to me so appropriate for you' (LT 193). As Thérèse ponders the scriptures, she comes to the point where she can say: 'a single word uncovers for my soul infinite horizons' (LT 226).

---

49 Testimony of Sr. Marie of Jesus, quoted in *La Bible, op. cit.*, p. 14.
50 See O'Donnell, *Prayer, op. cit.*, p. 81.

Surrender and trust

'Jesus deigned to show me the road that leads to this Divine Furnace,' Thérèse writes, speaking of the fire of love, 'and this road is the *surrender* of the little child who sleeps without fear in its Father's arms' (SS, p. 188). It took her years to achieve this total surrender, to walk in the way of absolute confidence and trust. The Lord seems to have kept her waiting and waiting, patiently. Then comes the breakthrough – 'in one instant' (SS, p. 98). This succinct phrase runs almost like a refrain throughout her writings (cf. SS, pp. 58, 97, 277; PN 17, stanza 6).

Thérèse's temperament did not take kindly to surrender. Her mother described the young Thérèse as a 'little imp', commenting: 'one doesn't know how things will go, she ... has a stubborn streak in her that is almost invincible' (SS, p. 22). These words were later echoed by her confessor: 'had [God] abandoned you, instead of being a little angel, you would have become a little demon' (SS, p. 149). After her sister Pauline entered Carmel, the young Thérèse, once so happy and carefree, became timid, scrupulous and more sensitive than ever, easily dissolving in tears, retiring and introspective. Eventually, she emerged from the struggle. She called this her 'complete conversion' (SS, p. 98). It was Christmas Eve: 'that luminous *night*,' she says, when 'Jesus ... changed the night of my soul into rays of light' (SS, p. 97). Thérèse comments significantly: 'The work I had been unable to do in ten years was done by Jesus in one instant' (SS, p. 98).

After Thérèse had spent three years in Carmel, she still agonised over her 'faults' and worried constantly about offending God. Then, during a retreat, the visiting priest who had spoken no more than a few words to her 'launched me full sail upon the waves of *confidence and love* which so strongly attracted me, but upon which I dared not advance' (SS, p. 174). Her surrender to God's action had now reached another significant turning-point in her life. Again, it happened in an instant. Her experience would take away the fear of death, for she well knew that God had transformed her in one moment and could do so again. Her *Act of Oblation* sums this up well, echoing and adapting the words of scripture: 'a single day is like a thousand years. You can, then, in one instant prepare me to appear before You' (SS, p. 277; cf. 2 Pt 3:8). In one of her poems, Thérèse writes: 'Living on Love is banishing every fear, / Every memory of past faults. / I see no imprint of my sins. / In a moment love has burned everything...' (PN 17, stanza 6).

We are fortunate to have many telling photographs of Thérèse. Conrad De Meester, a distinguished commentator on her life and works, uses the image of her hand to great effect. It describes well, he says, how her surrender gradually deepened:

> To use an analogy, we could say that, at first, her hand was held with palm downward and fingers clenched, seeking to grasp as best they could. Then, with the passage of time and a change of attitude and perspective, her fingers relaxed gradually and eventually released their hold, while her hand turned until her palm was outstretched, ready to offer and to receive much in return. It took Thérèse almost her entire lifetime to reach this point.[51]

The final testing

We discover the real cost of total surrender for Thérèse in the great and final testing of her faith. Shortly before her death, she wrote to a priest friend: 'my way is all confidence and love' (LT 226). But soon afterwards, she is writing about the 'thickest darkness' (SS, p. 211) which had invaded her soul fourteen months earlier. It was Easter. Thérèse had coughed up blood just a few days before. This was the first summons – a *distant murmur*', she called it, '*that announced the Bridegroom's arrival*' (SS, p. 211).

It is risky to assume that we can understand what Thérèse was experiencing at this time. She herself found it almost impossible to explain: 'One would have to travel through this dark tunnel to understand its darkness' (SS, p. 212), she wrote starkly. Or, as she expressed it again: she was covered in 'thick fog', which suddenly became 'more dense' (SS, pp. 213-4). Her torment redoubled. The psalmist, at his bleakest, expresses Thérèse's experience only too well: 'my one companion is darkness' (Ps 87:19). This darkness borrowed the voice of sinners and said to her, mockingly, that death would not give her what she hoped for, but only 'the night of nothingness' (SS, p. 213). She confided to one of her community: 'I don't believe in eternal life, it seems to me that after this mortal life there is nothing left... Everything has disappeared for me, love is all I have.'[52] She could not discern any trace of heaven. Everything, it seemed, had vanished. Even her own 'Little Way' seemed lost, swallowed up in its own littleness.

A month before Thérèse died, her sister Pauline was sitting by her bed. Thérèse pointed to the chestnut trees near the cemetery and said, 'Look! Do

---

51 Conrad De Meester, O.C.D., *With Empty Hands: The Message of St Thérèse of Lisieux*, (London & New York: Burns & Oates, 2002), p. 119.
52 A confidence made to Sr. Teresa of Saint Augustine: quoted in PN, p. 184.

you see the black hole where we can see nothing; it's in a similar hole that I am as far as body and soul are concerned. Ah! what darkness! But I am in peace' (LC, p. 173). Near the end, she confided that the pain was enough 'to make her lose her reason'. She asked her sister not to leave any poisonous medicines around her and said, 'If I had not had any faith, I would have committed suicide without an instant's hesitation' (LC, p. 196; cf. pp. 162-3). Earlier that summer, Thérèse had said, quoting Job: 'Although he should kill me, I will trust in him' (LC, p. 77; cf. Jb 13:15). That trust was tested in so many ways, not least by the uncertainty concerning her illness. Her doctors had given conflicting views. Thérèse was perplexed. Was death imminent? Or would this excruciating pain last for years? However, she refused to submit to anxiety. Her phrase 'everything is a grace' (LC, p. 57) sums up her response at all times. When she felt she could take no more, she said to the prioress who was at her bedside, 'I assure you, the chalice is filled to the brim!... But God is not going to abandon me, I'm sure... He has never abandoned me' (LC, p. 205). These words were uttered the day of her death: the ultimate trust.

Speaking the truth in love

Thérèse, we have seen, had no illusions about religious life. Nor did she have any illusions about the Church. She was of one mind with another future Doctor of the Church, Catherine of Siena, who felt that those are truly blessed who suffer at not seeing the Church as fair as they would like and are all the more faithful because of it. It is often assumed that criticism in the Church is a voice of the angry and disgruntled. It may be, but it is not necessarily so. Honest criticism is a function of love and was part of Thérèse's vision of church as communion, in which each member belongs fully, as family. 'I am the *Child of the Church*,' she said. 'I love the Church, my Mother!' (SS, pp. 196-7).

To avoid the challenge of speaking out is the easy option. But it was precisely her love for the Church that enabled Thérèse to discern things clearly, and unmask deception and pretence. She was to discover that criticism of this kind was 'a painful operation' but added: 'truth always wins out' (SS, p. 240). As a young religious, she became uneasy with the attachment which one of her companions had to the superior. Thérèse felt that she must act, in true love, to open the eyes of the young nun, even though it could be at some cost to herself.[53] One commentator has referred to this episode as 'a fight for truth'.[54] Thérèse writes: 'the moment had come and I must no longer fear to speak out...

---

53   Her sister Pauline had warned Thérèse that she might even be sent away, if the superior heard of it: see Gaucher, *op. cit.*, p. 123. For Thérèse's own description of the episode, see SS, pp. 235-7.
54   Gaucher, *op. cit.*, p. 122.

[I told this sister] *everything I was thinking about her*' (SS, p. 236). She followed the words of *Ephesians* (4:15) and told her companion the truth – with love. The young nun recognised that Thérèse's motives were genuine and took the lesson to heart. Thérèse would say later: 'If I'm not loved, that's just too bad! I tell the whole truth, and if anyone doesn't wish to know the truth, let her not come looking for me' (LC, p. 38).

It was the same sense of conviction that led Thérèse to voice constructive criticism wherever she found it necessary. She asked the unwilling superior that there be more frequent communion – a custom not yet accepted by the Carmel of Lisieux.[55] Thérèse also expresses the hurt which many women feel today with regard to the Church. She is not a strident voice, but is no less a challenge to the Church she loved so deeply. She recalls how she travelled in Italy as a young girl, and 'every minute someone was saying [to the women]: "Don't enter here! Don't enter there, you will be excommunicated!"' (SS, p. 140). In desperation, she releases her indignation:

> Ah! poor women, how they are misunderstood! And yet they love God in much larger numbers than men do and during the Passion of Our Lord, women had more courage than the apostles since they braved the insults of the soldiers and dared to dry the adorable Face of Jesus. It is undoubtedly because of this that He allows misunderstanding to be their lot on earth, since He chose it for Himself. In heaven, He will show that His thoughts are not men's thoughts, for then the *last will be first*. (SS, p. 140)

A fragile Church

There is considerable disappointment today at the discovery of clerical failings. Thérèse had a special love for priests but, observing them on the train to Rome, she records her shock upon seeing that they were 'weak and fragile men' who '[showed] in their conduct their extreme need for prayers' (SS, p. 122). To be human is an essential part of what it means to be a priest.[56] The priest is weak and fragile like Jesus, because like Jesus he is human. To exalt the priest above this shared humanity is to deny the incarnation: 'He can deal gently with the ignorant and wayward, since he himself is beset with weakness' (Heb 5:2). This is not to minimise in any way the clerical sins and glaring abuse of trust highlighted recently by the press and media. These failings have rightly

---

55 *Ibid.*, p. 190.
56 See the Carmelite journal *Mount Carmel*, vol. 52/3, 2004 – an issue devoted to the priesthood.

The shrine of Saint Thérèse in Whitefriar Street Carmelite Church, Dublin.

outraged, pained and angered many – not least the vast majority of priests themselves who are good, committed and often heroic in their service of the Church. However, much support and sympathy is still needed for the scarred victims and their families, as well as soul-searching by the Church, together with healing and reconciliation. The clerical voice must join the cry of the repentant Church to ask forgiveness for the wounds inflicted and suffered.

Peter was one of Thérèse's favourite gospel characters. She said that she could understand perfectly why he fell: 'he was relying upon himself instead of relying only upon God's strength ... Before Peter fell,' she reminds us, 'Our Lord had said to him: "And once you are converted, strengthen your brethren"' (LC, pp. 140-1). Then she proceeds to comment on what Jesus had said: 'This means: Convince them of the weakness of human strength through your own experience' (LC, p. 141). In the gospel, Jesus spoke these words to Peter: 'I have prayed for you that your faith may not fail' (Lk 22:32). Jesus did not pray that Peter himself would not fail. He is bound to fail, almost by definition, because he is human. Jesus prayed that Peter's *faith* might not fail, and so guaranteed the only permanent foundation of a community of believers: a Church supported in its weakness by the prayer of Jesus. Little wonder that the story of the Pharisee and the publican was a special favourite with Thérèse: 'He told this story to some who trusted in themselves that they were virtuous...' (Lk 18:9-14). She comments: 'I repeat, filled with confidence, the publican's humble prayer... Like the publican, I felt I was a great sinner. I found God to be so merciful!... My confidence is not lessened' (SS, p. 258; LC, p. 147). These words may surprise us. For as sinners go, Thérèse was not in the top league! She was not even in the ranks of the 'sinner' saints, Augustine and the Magdalen. But she did not miss the point of the parable: the opposite of sin is not virtue, it is God's grace, his merciful love. So, she can identify with the prayer of the publican: 'God, be merciful to me a sinner!' (Lk 18:13; cf. SS, p. 212).

Thérèse is now a 'Doctor of the Church'.[57] This confirms that her message is universal – that is, for the whole people of God. Her teaching provides all believers with a deeply scriptural way of living their faith in the full acceptance of human frailty. Thérèse also encourages a fragile and repentant Church to face the future with renewed trust in God's limitless mercy: 'Yes, I feel it; even though I had on my conscience all the sins that can be committed, I would go, my heart broken with sorrow, and throw myself into Jesus' arms ... I go to Him with confidence and love...' (SS, p. 259). These are the last words she ever wrote.[58]

---

57 See Steven Payne, O.C.D., *Saint Thérèse of Lisieux: Doctor of the Universal Church*, (New York: Alba House, 2002); Eugene McCaffrey, O.C.D., *Heart of Love: Saint Thérèse of Lisieux*, (Dublin: Veritas, 1998), pp. 74-9.
58 I am referring here to the last words of *Story of a Soul*, abandoned at the beginning of July 1897 because of her illness (see LC, p. 70); she did, however, write a few letters and prayers after this date.

This article first appeared in James McCaffrey, O.C.D., *Captive Flames: A Biblical Reading of the Carmelite Saints*, (Dublin: Veritas, 2005), and is reproduced here by kind permission of the author and publisher.

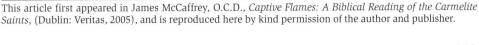

*Saints Brocard and Elijah scaling Mount Carmel, with saints
of the Carmelite Order flanking Our Lady and the Christ child below:
(left-right) John of the Cross, Thérèse of Lisieux, Simon Stock,
Teresa of Jesus. Icon written by the Carmelite nuns of Ravenna, Italy.*

An introduction to *Lectio Divina* meditation on the Scriptures

Joseph Chalmers, O.Carm.

When we pray, in some way we enter into a relationship with God. Prayer is our response to God who first approaches us. The *Catechism of the Catholic Church* understands prayer firstly as a relationship with God and only secondly as a special activity. Article 2558 says:

> "Great is the mystery of the faith!" The Church professes this mystery in the Apostles' Creed (*Part One*) and celebrates it in the sacramental liturgy (*Part Two*), so that the life of the faithful may be conformed to Christ in the Holy Spirit to the glory of God the Father (*Part Three*). This mystery, then, requires that the faithful believe in it, that they celebrate it, and that they live from it in a vital and personal relationship with the living and true God. This relationship is prayer.

Personal relationships take time, energy and a commitment in order to develop. We must find something in common with the other person. What we have in common with God is Jesus Christ. He is the culmination of all that God has done for the world, and in Christ can be found everything that God wants to say to humanity. In the Scriptures we read the story of how God spoke to the people and what God wants to say. The whole of Scripture leads us to the fullness of the revelation of God in Christ Jesus. We cannot say that we want to know God if we ignore the divine message in Sacred Scripture. There is always something new to discover in the Scriptures.

The rediscovery of the centrality of the Word of God in the Church led to the rediscovery also of the ancient practice of *Lectio Divina* (holy reading). This was the normal way of prayer of the ancient monks and from them passed on to all the older religious orders. This way of prayer has had a profound effect on the history of Christian spirituality and can be said to be a constant in the Christian life. *Lectio Divina* is not only a method of prayer, but is a way of life; it is not simply yet another thing to be fitted in to our already overcrowded schedules, but rather is the element that shapes our whole day according to the will of God. It is, in fact, the form of all Christian prayer.

According to an ancient tradition, there are four fundamental moments in this way of prayer: Reading, Meditation, Prayer and Contemplation. Or to put these another way: Read, Reflect, Respond and Rest. These moments are not strictly separated but flow into each other naturally and other moments can be added. Prayer is a very personal thing and each person must follow where the Spirit leads. The four traditional moments of *Lectio Divina* are simply an indication of the basic elements that make up Christian prayer.

Prayer is rather like soup. Good soup (prayer) has these four elements as basic ingredients, but each cook will have a different recipe. The soup will have a different taste according to the quantity of each ingredient and according to what other ingredients are added. We have a great freedom in our relationship with God but *Lectio Divina* contains the wisdom of centuries of living the Christian life. *Lectio Divina* is not a rigid method but changes according to the person who follows its rhythm.

Read

The first ingredient is **Lectio** (the traditional name), or, in other words, a time to read the Word of God. We can read the Scriptures in many ways. With the rosary "we read" the Word of God in the sense that the prayers come from the Sacred Scriptures. Looking at frescoes and stained glass windows was the way in which uneducated people in the Middle Ages could "read" the Scriptures. Of course these things can still speak very powerfully to us today. The same can be said for statues, tapestries and any way of telling the biblical stories. We can read the Sacred Scriptures during daily Mass and in the Prayer of the Church, the Office. To read the Word of God with profit, we must listen attentively in order to receive what God wants to give us. Clearly it is not sufficient to listen to the Word; we must also put it into practice, as Mary the mother of Jesus did (cf. *Luke* 11:27-28). It is possible to listen to the Scriptures in a perfunctory fashion without allowing the words to touch us. It is necessary to make an effort to receive what God wants to say to us at each moment.

The Word of God is the story of God's relationship with the human family; it is the story of my and your relationship with God. We learn from the Old and New Testaments how God speaks to us and what are the problems inherent in this dialogue. By means of the Word, God speaks personally to you and to me. God wants to say something particular to us, and if we do not listen we will not receive this very important message. When we read the Scriptures, it is necessary to take time, lest the Word goes in one ear and out the other without touching our hearts. It is important to reserve every day a little time to read or listen to the Word of God.

A statue of Thérèse in front of her Basilica in Lisieux.

If one stops praying, it is difficult to get back into a rhythm. Although it is not necessary to be rigid in the exact time set aside, it is a commitment that must not be forgotten if we want to maintain a healthy relationship with God. There will also be days when all our plans are thrown into confusion and we hardly have time to bless ourselves. On those occasions we can say something like, "Today, Lord, I am really busy. Perhaps I will forget you. Please do not forget me!" However, these occasions must be an exception to the normal rhythm of our personal relationship with God.

Reflect

The second moment or ingredient of *Lectio Divina* is **meditatio**. This term, which means meditation, is very wide and so it is necessary to define it a little. In our western European tradition, to meditate is equivalent to reflect on God or on the things of God. In Buddhism, on the contrary it means "not thinking", and includes the various techniques used to arrive at this. Because of the influence of eastern religious practices, the normally accepted meaning of meditation in the world at large is this, and in particular because of the widespread use of "transcendental meditation". However there also remains the traditional idea of reflecting on God or on some point of our faith. In this type of meditation we try to enter more profoundly into the mystery of God or the mysteries of the faith. For example, we can spend a little time thinking about the Eucharist, starting from a text of Scripture. Then we could think about what the Eucharist means for us today. We receive Christ as our food so that we might begin to live like him. This is only one example among many of a meditation. We have a brain and we must use it also in the area of our faith life.

There is another type of meditation, more ancient than that described above. At the beginnings of Christianity, meditation involved the whole body. When the first Carmelite hermits lived on Mount Carmel in the early 13th century they understood meditation as a method for affixing the words of Sacred Scripture – and especially the psalms – in the mind and heart. Every hermit repeated the scriptural words over and over, with special emphasis on the psalms, in a loud voice. That is probably one reason their cells were originally quite far apart so that each would not be disturbed by the noise of the other. Gradually it was hoped that the Word of God would transform their hearts.

Meditation, then, can have for us today also these different meanings: to reflect on the Word of God in order to apply it to one's own life, or repeat the words slowly in order to fix them in the heart. What does this Word say to me today, or what does the Lord want to say to me at this particular moment?

It can be useful to consult a Bible commentary to find a brief explanation of the chosen text. For the person of faith these comments help the reader to enter more easily into the Word of God presented by these ancient stories. It is not necessary to spend much time studying the text, but it is important to take a moment in order to get an idea of what God really is saying and so avoid the risk of making the Word say what we want to hear.

Respond

The third traditional moment or ingredient of *Lectio Divina* is **oratio**, which means prayer. This is our response to the Word of God. You may wonder has not everything we have been doing up to this point not also been prayer? Of course. However, according to the ancient monks from whom we have received *Lectio Divina*, prayer was understood as an opportunity for a heart-to-heart dialogue with God. The two previous moments – reading the Word and reflecting on it – are really a preparation for this intimate conversation with God. This intimate dialogue can take place in the midst of our normal daily tasks and can easily interchange with moments of meditation. For example, while we are working we could perhaps think about the passage of Scripture that we had chosen, or, like the monks of antiquity, we might choose to repeat some word or phrase so that the Word of God might take hold of our heart. We have to adapt ourselves to the circumstances of our lives. These words or our thoughts are aimed at touching our heart and starting a real dialogue with God. The conversation with the Lord can take many forms and is very personal. If it starts to rain and you are caught without an umbrella, your prayer might be one of complaint. If you are very worried, your prayer will probably focus on what you are worried about. You can praise or thank God. The psalms cover the whole spectrum of human emotion and they teach us that we can speak with God about anything. The goal of *Lectio Divina* is to open the human heart to God so that it might be transformed.

Spontaneous prayer sooner or later tends to diminish and silence becomes more and more normal. In the silence we leave a space for the Spirit of God to pray in us. Scripture says: "The Spirit too comes to help us in our weakness, for, when we do not know how to pray properly, then the Spirit personally makes our petitions for us in groans that cannot be put into words; and he who can see into all hearts knows what the Spirit means because the prayers that the Spirit makes for God's holy people are always in accordance with the mind of God." (*Romans* 8:26-27).

Rest

The traditional name for the fourth moment or ingredient of *Lectio Divina* is **contemplatio** or contemplation. This is a concept with a lot of history behind it and not a few difficulties connected to it. I prefer to use a more common term that is easily understandable: rest. At this point we are invited to enter into the mystery of God. It is no longer necessary to think holy thoughts, or to speak but simply to rest in God. "Come to me, all you who labour and are overburdened, and I will give you rest. Shoulder my yoke and learn from me, for I am gentle and humble in heart, and you will find rest for your souls. Yes, my yoke is easy and my burden light." (*Matthew* 11:28-30).

When our prayer becomes silence, perhaps it may seem that we are wasting time. There will be a temptation to return to a form of prayer where we were in control, or at least where we had the sensation of doing something. However, silence is a normal development of prayer. There comes a time when we must leave behind our beautiful words because they cannot express what is in our heart. In silence, God can listen to what is in our heart and we can listen to the still small voice of God.

According to the *Catechism of the Catholic Church*:

> **2712** Contemplative prayer is the prayer of the child of God, of the forgiven sinner who agrees to welcome the love by which he is loved and who wants to respond to it by loving even more. But he knows that the love he is returning is poured out by the Spirit in his heart, for everything is grace from God. Contemplative prayer is the poor and humble surrender to the loving will of the Father in ever deeper union with his beloved Son.

2713 Contemplative prayer is the simplest expression of the mystery of prayer. It is a gift, a grace; it can be accepted only in humility and poverty. Contemplative prayer is a covenant relationship established by God within our hearts. Contemplative prayer is a *communion* in which the Holy Trinity conforms man, the image of God, "to his likeness."

2714 Contemplative prayer is also the pre-eminently intense time of prayer. In it the Father strengthens our inner being with power through his Spirit "that Christ may dwell in [our] hearts through faith" and we may be "grounded in love."

2715 Contemplation is a *gaze* of faith, fixed on Jesus. "I look at him and he looks at me": this is what a certain peasant of Ars used to say to his holy curé about his prayer before the tabernacle. This focus on Jesus is a renunciation of self. His gaze purifies our heart; the light of the countenance of Jesus illumines the eyes of our heart and teaches us to see everything in the light of his truth and his compassion for all men. Contemplation also turns its gaze on the mysteries of the life of Christ. Thus it learns the "interior knowledge of our Lord," the more to love him and follow him.

2716 Contemplative prayer is *hearing* the Word of God. Far from being passive, such attentiveness is the obedience of faith, the unconditional acceptance of a servant, and the loving commitment of a child. It participates in the "Yes" of the Son become servant and the Fiat of God's lowly handmaid.

2717 Contemplative prayer is *silence*, the "symbol of the world to come" or "silent love." Words in this kind of prayer are not speeches; they are like kindling that feeds the fire of love. In this silence, unbearable to the "outer" man, the Father speaks to us his incarnate Word, who suffered, died, and rose; in this silence the Spirit of adoption enables us to share in the prayer of Jesus.

2718 Contemplative prayer is a union with the prayer of Christ insofar as it makes us participate in his mystery. The mystery of Christ is celebrated by the Church in the Eucharist, and the Holy Spirit makes it come alive in contemplative prayer so that our charity will manifest it in our acts.

2719 Contemplative prayer is a communion of love bearing Life for the multitude, to the extent that it consents to abide in the night of faith. The Paschal night of the Resurrection passes through the night of the agony and the tomb – the three intense moments of the Hour of Jesus which his Spirit (and not "the flesh [which] is weak") brings to life in prayer. We must be willing to "keep watch with [him] one hour."

When we read the Word of God, or meditate on it or pray about it, we are using our own words and thoughts, but the Word belongs to God and possibly God wants to comment on it. God often does this by inspiring a thought or a feeling. The ancient monks believed that it was important to leave some time for God, and they called this time *contemplatio* (contemplation). Many people can be rather suspicious of this word. By calling cloistered nuns "contemplatives" we may often think that we can leave contemplation to them. However if we translate the word "contemplation" by another term like, "an intimate relationship with God in Jesus Christ", we can perhaps begin to see that it cannot be exclusive to cloistered nuns. Contemplation is for everyone.

The fruit of prayer is not the brilliant ideas that we may have about Scripture or the feelings of love that rise up in our heart. At times it is impossible to have a single holy thought. The fruit of prayer can only be seen outside the time of prayer in the way we relate with others on a regular basis. If our prayer is authentic, our life will begin to change, probably not in extraordinary ways, but in the small details of daily life. It is quite possible that we ourselves may not be at all aware of any of these changes, but they will begin to strike those with whom we live and work.

We need some quiet time when we leave behind our own words, thoughts, and ideas and simply rest in God, who loves us with a love that goes beyond anything we would imagine. At the end of this chapter I suggest a method of silent prayer dubbed 'Prayer in Secret'. This method is based above all on the work of Fr. Thomas Keating, O.C.S.O.[1] It is a method that helps one move from the third phase of *Lectio Divina*, that of responding to God in spontaneous prayer (*oratio*) in order to simply wait for God in silence, so that we will be

---

1   *Open Mind, Open Heart*, (Massachusetts: Element Books, 1992). For a simple introduction to this method of prayer and its background, see Elizabeth Smith and Joseph Chalmers, *A Deeper Love*, (Tunbridge Wells, Kent: Burns & Oates, and New York: Continuum, 1999).

ready when and if God wishes to bring us into greater depths. This method can be a preparation for contemplative prayer (*contemplatio*).

Act

Finally we can add a fifth moment or ingredient of *Lectio Divina*: *actio* (action), which is also important because it moves prayer into daily life. The goal of Christian prayer is to enter into an intimate relationship with God but this process must have effects in daily life. According to the *First letter of John*:

> My dear friends, let us love one another, since love is from God and everyone who loves is a child of God and knows God. Whoever fails to love does not know God, because God is love. This is the revelation of God's love for us, that God sent his only Son into the world that we might have life through him. Love consists in this: it is not we who loved God, but God loved us and sent his Son to expiate our sins. My dear friends, if God loved us so much, we too should love one another. No one has ever seen God, but as long as we love one another God remains in us and his love comes to its perfection in us. (*I John* 4:7-12).

The example of Saint Thérèse can help us to remain faithful to God in times that are not always easy. Let us journey together with her to Christ, the Word of God.

Prayer in secret

Lectio Divina is the most traditional way of growing in an intimate relationship with God and it is through this relationship that we are transformed and made capable of living the Gospel in all its fullness. A monk of the 12th century has described the key moments of *Lectio Divina*: read the Word; reflect on the Word (meditate); respond to the Word (prayer during which we allow our hearts to spontaneously turn towards God); and rest in the Word (contemplation). The key moments are not rigid points to be followed one after the other but are descriptions of the way prayer normally develops, with one flowing into the other. There are some methods to help us when we begin to experience that all our words and thoughts are no longer sufficient. We may feel a call to silence but we do not know what to do.

I want to propose a method of prayer which can make silence very fruitful and can help us wait for God in silence. It is a method of Christian prayer that is based on the very rich contemplative tradition and especially on a classic book of this tradition called *The Cloud of Unknowing* written anonymously in the 14th century.[2] I am not suggesting that one should leave other personal ways of prayer, but this method could deepen these other methods and make them even more fruitful. The most important thing for this way of prayer is to be convinced that God is not far away but is very close. God is at home within us (cf. *John* 14:23).

This method of prayer is usually called *Centering Prayer* but could also be called the *prayer of silence* or the *prayer of desire* because in the silence we stretch out towards God with our desire.[3] It has also been called *prayer in secret*, following Jesus' counsel to go into one's private room and to pray to the Father in secret (*Matthew* 6:6).[4]

The first phase of this prayer is to find a suitable place where the interruptions will be reduced to a minimum. Then get into a comfortable position that you can hold without fidgeting for the whole time of the prayer. Usually a minimum of 20 minutes is recommended.

One can begin this prayer with a short reading from the Bible. Now is not the time to think about the meaning of the words; that kind of meditation is for another time. Now is the time simply to be in the presence of God and consent to the divine action with our intention. Then, with eyes closed, introduce very gently a sacred word into your heart. A sacred word is a word that is very significant for you in your ongoing relationship with God. For example, the little word "yes" can mean a lot of things. "Do you want an ice cream?" "Yes". Or "Will you marry me?" "Yes". Such a little word can mean very little or a great deal and can change the whole of your life. In a close relationship two people can use pet-names for each other that may sound rather silly to outsiders but are highly significant to those involved in the relationship. The sacred word, then, should be sacred for you. According to the teaching of *The Cloud of Unknowing* it is better if this word be very brief, one syllable if possible.[5] I can suggest some possible words:

---

2   *Cloud of Unknowing and Other Works,* translated by Clifton Wolters, (London: Penguin Books, 1961).

3   Centering Prayer was taught originally by three Trappist monks in the U.S.A. who had made a profound study of the Christian contemplative tradition. Fr. Basil Pennington has written many books, such as *Centering Prayer* (London / New York / Sydney: Image Book, Doubleday, 1980). Fr. William Menninger has concentrated more on *The Cloud of Unknowing*; see his *The Loving Search for God* (New York: Continuum, 1994). The basic book to learn more about this way of prayer remains that of Fr. Thomas Keating, *Open Mind, Open Heart* (Massachusetts: Element Books, 1992). For a simple introduction to Centering Prayer and its background see Elizabeth Smith & Joseph Chalmers, *A Deeper Love*, (Tunbridge Wells, Kent: Burns & Oates, and New York: Continuum, 1999).

4   See Thomas Keating, *Manifesting God*, (New York: Lantern Books, 2005).

5   *Cloud of Unknowing* (op. cit.) chapter 7, p. 69.

"God"

"Lord"

"Love"

"Jesus"

"Spirit"

"Father"

"Mary"

"Yes"

Choose a word that is most significant for you. Perhaps one will come to you if you ask God's help.

When I said to introduce the sacred word into your heart, I am not suggesting that you pronounce it with your lips or even mentally, but rather welcome it within you without thinking of its meaning. It is not necessary to force the sacred word. It should be very gentle. The sacred word is not a mantra to be constantly repeated. The word focuses our desire and we use it always in the same way simply to return our heart to the Lord as soon as we become aware that we are distracted. This is a prayer of *intention* and not *attention*. Our intention is to be in the presence of God and to consent to the divine action in our lives. The sacred word expresses this intention, and so when we become aware that we are thinking of something else we can decide either to continue with the distraction because we find it more interesting or return to our intention to be in the presence of God and consent to what God wants to accomplish in us. We return our heart to God by the very gentle use of the sacred word. It is a symbol of our intention. It is not necessary to repeat it frequently but only when we wish to return our heart to God.

During this prayer it is not the time to talk to God with beautiful words or even to have holy thoughts, even if we think that these are inspirations from God. These things are best left for another moment. Our silence and our desire are worth far more than many words.

By means of the word that we have chosen, we express our desire and our intention to remain in the presence of God and to consent to the purifying and transforming divine action. We return to the sacred word, which is the symbol of our intention and our desire, only when we become aware that we are involved in something else. The prayer consists simply in being in the presence of God without thinking of anything in particular. It is a prayer of relationship with God – Father, Son and Holy Spirit. If you understand how to be in silence with another person without thinking or doing anything in particular, then you will be able to understand what this prayer is all about. This method of prayer is not for everyone. If you feel an interior call to greater silence, it may be of help to you.

At the end of the period that you have decided to dedicate to prayer, perhaps you can say an *Our Father* or other prayer very slowly. It is good to remain in silence for a few moments in order to prepare yourself to bring the fruit of your prayer into your daily life.

Let's summarise the simple steps for this method of prayer...

Practical guidelines for Centering Prayer or the Prayer in Secret

There are four simple guidelines to this method of prayer.[6]

1. Choose a sacred word as the symbol of your intention to consent to the presence and action of God within.

2. Sitting comfortably and with eyes closed, settle briefly and then silently introduce the sacred word as the symbol of your consent to God's presence and action within.

3. When engaged with your thoughts, return ever so gently to the sacred word.

4. At the end of the prayer period, remain in silence with eyes closed for a couple of minutes.

---

6   See Thomas Keating, *Manifesting God,* pp. 133-139.

This chapter is adapted from Joseph Chalmers, *The Sound of Silence – Listening to the Word of God with the Prophet Elijah,* (Faversham: Saint Albert's Press, 2007).

Sculpture of Thérèse at the Carmel in Lourdes.

Saint Thérèse – infused with the Word of God

In her writings and conversations, Saint Thérèse quoted from the Bible more than a thousand times. A few selected examples are provided here to show how closely Thérèse modelled her words and life on the words and life of Jesus Christ, her Master and Brother, as well as his precursors and disciples. These passages from God's living Word set alongside the thoughts of Thérèse may prompt reflection about your own relationship with God. In a spirit of *Lectio Divina*, you might like to reflect on Holy Scripture in the company of Saint Thérèse.

Bible quotations are from the *New Revised Standard Version*. Quotations from Thérèse are from her autobiography, *Story of a Soul* (abbreviated as *SS*, followed by page reference to the 1976 I.C.S. Publications Second Edition), and from *Her Last Conversations* (abbreviated *LC*, with page references from the I.C.S. edition of 1977). Both these publications include a Biblical index, making it easy for you to look up the context for occasions when Thérèse quoted directly or indirectly from Scripture. Scriptural references can also be found in the letters and poems of St. Thérèse, both printed by I.C.S. Publications.

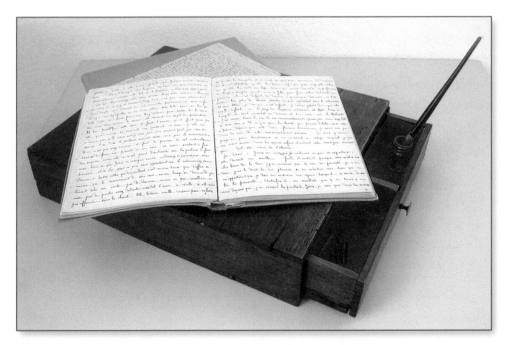

One of the writing desks used in the Carmel at Lisieux.

From Thérèse of Lisieux, *Story of a Soul*	
I will sing of your steadfast love, O Lord, for ever; with my mouth I will proclaim your faithfulness to all generations. I declare that your steadfast love is established for ever; your faithfulness is as firm as the heavens. *Psalm* 89 (88):1-2	I shall begin to sing what I must sing eternally: 'The Mercies of the Lord' SS p. 13
The Lord is merciful and gracious, slow to anger and abounding in steadfast love. *Psalm* 103 (102):8	To me the Lord has always been 'merciful and good, slow to anger and abounding in steadfast love'. SS p. 15
'I tell you, I will never again drink of this fruit of the vine until that day when I drink it new with you in my Father's kingdom.' *Matthew* 26:29	Alas, poor little Mother was already too sick to eat the fruits of the earth; she was to be satisfied only in heaven with God's glory and was to drink the mysterious wine He spoke about at the Last Supper, saying He would share it with us in His Father's Kingdom. SS p. 33
But when Jesus heard it [the news of Lazarus's sickness], he said, 'This illness does not lead to death; rather it is for God's glory, so that the Son of God may be glorified through it.' *John* 11:4	I had a very serious illness... This sickness was not 'unto death', but like that of Lazarus it was to give glory to God. SS p. 61
Upon my bed at night I sought him whom my soul loves; I sought him, but found him not; I called him, but he gave no answer. *Song of Songs* 3:1	The morning of the day I was to visit [the Carmelites] I was thinking things over in my bed (for it was there I made my profound meditations, and, contrary to the bride in the Canticles, I always found my Beloved there). SS p. 71
When you give alms, do not let your left hand know what your right hand is doing, so that your alms may be done in secret; and your Father who sees in secret will reward you. *Matthew* 6:3-4	Soon God made me feel that true glory is that which will lasts eternally, and to reach it, it isn't necessary to perform striking works but to hide oneself and practice virtue in such a way that the left hand knows not what the right is doing. SS p. 72
Then I considered all that my hands had done and the toil I had spent in doing it, and again, all was vanity and a chasing after wind, and there was nothing to be gained under the sun. *Ecclesiastes* 2:11	I see that all is vanity and vexation of spirit under the sun, that the only good is to love God with all one's heart and to be poor in spirit here on earth. SS p. 73

Go and learn what this means, "I desire mercy, not sacrifice." For I have come to call not the righteous but sinners.' *Matthew* 9:13	Well, I am this child, the object of the foreseeing love of a Father who has not sent His Word to save the just, but sinners. *SS* p. 84
O my dove, in the clefts of the rock, in the covert of the cliff, let me see your face, let me hear your voice. *Song of Songs* 2:14	Jesus knew how weak I was and it was for this reason He hid me first in the crevice of the rock. *SS* p. 93
Simon answered, 'Master, we have worked all night long but have caught nothing. Yet if you say so, I will let down the nets.' *Luke* 5:5	The work I had been unable to do in ten years was done by Jesus in one instant, contenting himself with my good will which was never lacking. I could say to Him like His apostles: 'Master, I fished all night and caught nothing'. *SS* p. 99
After this, when Jesus knew that all was now finished, he said (in order to fulfil the scripture), 'I am thirsty'. *John* 19:28	The cry of Jesus on the Cross sounded continually in my heart: 'I thirst!' *SS* p. 99
As it is written, 'What no eye has seen, nor ear heard, nor the human heart conceived, what God has prepared for those who love him' – these things God has revealed to us through the Spirit; for the Spirit searches everything, even the depths of God. *1 Corinthians* 2:9-10 I consider that the sufferings of this present time are not worth comparing with the glory about to be revealed to us. *Romans* 8:18	I experienced already what God reserved for those who love Him (not with the eye but with the heart), and seeing the eternal rewards had no proportion to life's small sacrifices, I wanted to love, to love Jesus with a passion, giving him a thousand proofs of my love while it was possible. *SS* p. 102
At that time Jesus said, 'I thank you, Father, Lord of heaven and earth, because you have hidden these things from the wise and the intelligent and have revealed them to infants'. *Matthew* 11:25	He, who cried out in His mortal life 'I thank thee, Father, that thou hast hidden these things from the wise and the prudent and revealed them to babes', willed to have His mercy shine out in me. *SS* p. 105
For I am convinced that neither death, nor life, nor angels, nor rulers, nor things present, nor things to come, nor powers, nor height, nor depth, nor anything else in all creation, will be able to separate us from the love of God in Christ Jesus our Lord. *Romans* 8:38-39	My heaven was none other than Love, and I felt, as did St. Paul, that nothing could separate us from the Divine Being who so ravished me! *SS* p. 112

You shall leave your name to my chosen to use as a curse, and the Lord God will put you to death; but to his servants he will give a different name. *Isaiah* 65:15 To everyone who conquers I will give some of the hidden manna, and I will give a white stone, and on the white stone is written a new name that no one knows except the one who receives it. *Revelation* 2:17	I understood true greatness is to be found in the soul, not in a name, since as Isaias says: 'The Lord will call his servants by ANOTHER NAME', and St. John says: 'To him that overcomes I will give a white stone, and on the stone a NEW NAME written which no man knows but the one who receives it.' *SS* p. 121
Do not be afraid, little flock, for it is your Father's good pleasure to give you the kingdom. *Luke* 12:32 I confer on you, just as my Father has conferred on me, a kingdom. *Luke* 22:29 Was it not necessary that the Messiah should suffer these things and then enter into his glory? *Luke* 24:26 And Jesus said to her, 'What do you want?' She said to him, 'Declare that these two sons of mine will sit, one at your right hand and one at your left, in your kingdom.' But Jesus answered, 'You do not know what you are asking. Are you able to drink the cup that I am about to drink?' *Matthew* 20:21-22	I was filled with confidence, for the Gospel of the day contained these beautiful words: 'Fear not, little flock, for it is your Father's good pleasure to give you the kingdom.' No, I did not fear, I hoped the kingdom of Carmel would soon belong to me; I was not thinking then of those other words of Jesus: 'And I appoint to you a kingdom even as my Father has appointed to me...' In other words, I reserve crosses and trials for you, and it is thus you will be worthy of possessing this kingdom after which you long; since it was necessary that the Christ suffer and that He enter through it into His glory, if you desire to have a place by His side, then drink the chalice He has drunk! *SS* p. 133
For my thoughts are not your thoughts, nor are your ways my ways, says the Lord. For as the heavens are higher than the earth, so are my ways higher than your ways and my thoughts than your thoughts. *Isaiah* 55:8-9 So the last will be first, and the first will be last. *Matthew* 20:16	Ah! poor women, how they are misunderstood! ... Our Lord allows misunderstanding to be their lot on earth, since He chose it for Himself. In heaven, He will show this His thoughts are not men's thoughts, for then the last will be first. *SS* p. 140

At that time Jesus said, 'I thank you, Father, Lord of heaven and earth, because you have hidden these things from the wise and the intelligent and have revealed them to infants'. *Matthew* 11:25	My heart quickly turned to the Director of directors, and it was He [Jesus] who taught me that science hidden from the wise and prudent and revealed to little ones. *SS* p. 151
As a father has compassion for his children, so the Lord has compassion for those who fear him. For he knows how we were made; he remembers that we are dust. *Psalm* 103 (102):13-14	I should be desolate for having slept (for seven years) during my hours of prayer and my thanksgivings after Holy Communion; well, I am not desolate. I remember that little children are as pleasing to their parents when they are asleep as well as when they are wide awake... I remember that 'The Lord knows our weakness, that he is mindful that we are but dust and ashes'. *SS* p. 165
For God is a God not of disorder but of peace *1 Corinthians* 14:33	Mother Geneviève said "Wait, my little child, I'm going to say just a little word to you... remember, my child, *Our God is a God of peace.*" *SS* p. 169
Then I considered all that my hands had done and the toil I had spent in doing it, and again, all was vanity and a chasing after wind, and there was nothing to be gained under the sun. *Ecclesiastes* 2:11	Jesus hidden also in this poor little heart was pleased to show it that everything is vanity and affliction of spirit under the sun. *SS* p. 175
Once Jesus was asked by the Pharisees when the kingdom of God was coming, and he answered, 'The kingdom of God is not coming with things that can be observed; nor will they say, "Look, here it is!" or "There it is!" For, in fact, the kingdom of God is within you.' *Luke* 17:20-21	It is especially the Gospels which sustain me during my hours of prayer, for in them I find what is necessary for my poor little soul. I am constantly discovering in them new lights, hidden and mysterious meanings. I understand and I know from experience that: 'The kingdom of God is within you'. *SS* p. 179
O give thanks to the Lord, for he is good; his steadfast love endures for ever! *Psalm* 118 (117):1	After so many graces can I not sing with the Psalmist: "How GOOD is the Lord, his MERCY endures forever!" *SS* p. 180
Then the father said to him [the brother of the prodigal son], "Son, you are always with me, and all that is mine is yours. *Luke* 15:31	What should I fear then? Ah! must not the infinitely just God, who deigns to pardon the faults of the prodigal son with so much kindness, be just also towards me who "am with Him always"? *SS* p. 180

Your steadfast love, O Lord, extends to the heavens, your faithfulness to the clouds. Your righteousness is like the mighty mountains, your judgements are like the great deep; you save humans and animals alike, O Lord. *Psalm* 36 (35):5-6	It seems to me that if You were to find souls offering themselves as victims of holocaust to Your Love, You would consume them rapidly; it seems to me, too, that You would be happy not to hold back the waves of infinite tenderness within You. If Your Justice loves to release itself, this Justice *which extends only over the earth*, how much more does Your Merciful Love desire to *set souls on fire* since Your Mercy *reaches to the heavens.* *SS* p. 181
Many waters cannot quench love, neither can floods drown it. If one offered for love all the wealth of one's house, it would be utterly scorned. *Song of Songs* 8:7 Wisdom says 'You that are simple, turn in here!' *Proverbs* 9:4 For the lowliest may be pardoned in mercy, but the mighty will be mightily tested. For the Lord of all will not stand in awe of anyone, or show deference to greatness; because he himself made both small and great, and he takes thought for all alike. *Wisdom* 6:6-7 He will feed his flock like a shepherd; he will gather the lambs in his arms, and carry them in his bosom, and gently lead the mother sheep. *Isaiah* 40:11 For thus says the Lord: I will extend prosperity to her like a river, and the wealth of the nations like an overflowing stream; and you shall nurse and be carried on her arm, and dandled on her knees. As a mother comforts her child, so I will comfort you; you shall be comforted in Jerusalem. *Isaiah* 66:12-13	The science of Love, ah, yes, this word resounds sweetly in the ear of my soul, and I desire only this science. *Having given all my riches for it,* I esteem it *as having given nothing* as did the bride in the sacred Canticles. I understand so well that this love is the only good I ambition. Jesus deigned to show me the road that leads to this Divine Furnace, and this road is the *surrender* of the little child who sleeps without fear in its Father's arms. "Whoever is a *little one*, let him come to me." So speaks the Holy Spirit through the mouth of Solomon. This same Spirit of Love also says: "*For to him that is little, mercy will be shown.*" The Prophet Isaias reveals in His name that on the last day: "*God shall feed his flock like a shepherd; he shall gather together the lambs with his arm, and shall take them up in his bosom.*" As though these promises were not sufficient, the same prophet whose gaze was already plunged into the eternal depths cried out in the Lord's name: "*As one whom a mother caresses, so will I comfort you; you shall be carried at the breasts and upon the knees they will caress you.*" *SS* p. 188

So Jesus came to a Samaritan city called Sychar, near the plot of ground that Jacob had given to his son Joseph. Jacob's well was there, and Jesus, tired out by his journey, was sitting by the well. It was about noon. A Samaritan woman came to draw water, and Jesus said to her, 'Give me a drink'. *John* 4:5-7	See, then, all that Jesus lays claim to from us; He has no need of our works but only of our *love*, for the same God who declares He *has no need to tell us when He is hungry* did not fear *to beg* for a little water from the Samaritan woman. He was thirsty. But when He said: *"Give me to drink,"* it was the *love* of His poor creature the Creator of the universe was seeking. He was thirsty for love. *SS* p. 189
It is good to conceal the secret of a king, but to acknowledge and reveal the works of God, and with fitting honour to acknowledge him. Do good, and evil will not overtake you. *Tobit* 12:7	How fortunate we are, dear Sister, to understand the intimate secrets of our Spouse. Ah! if you wished to write all you know about these secrets, we would have beautiful pages to read, but I know you prefer to keep *"the King's secrets"* in the bottom of your heart. And yet you say to me *"it is honourable to publish the works of the Most High"*. *SS* p. 189
And I saw the dead, great and small, standing before the throne, and books were opened. Also another book was opened, the book of life. And the dead were judged according to their works, as recorded in the books. *Revelation* 20:12	Jesus, Jesus, if I wanted to write all my desires, I would have to borrow Your *Book of Life*, for in it are reported all the actions of all the saints, and I would accomplish all of them for You. *SS* p. 193
Are all apostles? Are all prophets? Are all teachers? Do all work miracles? *1 Corinthians* 12:29 The eye cannot say to the hand, 'I have no need of you', nor again the head to the feet, 'I have no need of you.' *1 Corinthians* 12:21 But strive for the greater gifts. And I will show you a still more excellent way. If I speak in the tongues of mortals and of angels, but do not have love, I am a noisy gong or a clanging cymbal. *1 Corinthians* 12:31 - 13:1	During my meditation, my desires caused me a veritable martyrdom, and I opened the Epistles of St. Paul to find some kind of answer. Chapters 12 and 13 of the First Epistle to the Corinthians fell under my eyes. I read there, in the first of these chapters, that *all* cannot be apostles, prophets, doctors, etc., that the Church is composed of different members, and that the eye cannot be the hand *at one and the same time...* Without becoming discouraged, I continued my reading, and this sentence consoled me: *"Yet strive after THE BETTER GIFTS, and I point out to you a yet more excellent way."* And the Apostles explains how all *the most PERFECT gifts* are nothing without *LOVE*. *SS* pp. 193-94

I tell you, make friends for yourselves by means of dishonest wealth so that when it is gone, they may welcome you into the eternal homes. *Luke* 16:9 And his master commended the dishonest manager because he had acted shrewdly; for the children of this age are more shrewd in dealing with their own generation than are the children of light. *Luke* 16:8 When they had crossed, Elijah said to Elisha, 'Tell me what I may do for you, before I am taken from you.' Elisha said, 'Please let me inherit a double share of your spirit.' *2 Kings* 2:9	O Jesus, I know it, love is repaid by love alone, and so I searched and I found the way to solace my heart by giving you Love for Love. "Make use of the riches which render one unjust in order to make friends who will receive you into everlasting dwellings." Behold, Lord, the counsel You give Your disciples after having told them that "The children of this world, in relation to their own generation, are more prudent than are the children of the light." A child of light, I understood that *my desires of being everything*, or embracing all vocations, were the riches that would be able to render me unjust, so I made use of them *to make friends*. Remembering the prayer of Eliseus [Elisha] to his Father Elias [Elijah] when he dared to ask him for HIS DOUBLE SPIRIT, I presented myself before and angels and saints... *SS* p. 195
As an eagle stirs up its nest, and hovers over its young; as it spreads its wings, takes them up, and bears them aloft on its pinions, the Lord alone guided him; no foreign god was with him. *Deuteronomy* 32:11-12	Jesus, I am too little to perform great actions, and my own *folly* is this: to trust Your Love will accept me as a victim. My *folly* consists in begging the eagles, my brothers, to obtain for me the favour of flying towards the Sun of Love with the *Divine Eagle's own wings!* *SS* p. 200
O God, from my youth you have taught me, and I still proclaim your wondrous deeds. So even to old age and grey hairs, O God, do not forsake me, until I proclaim your might to all the generations to come. *Psalm* 71(70):17-18 For a thousand years in your sight are like yesterday when it is past, or like a watch in the night. *Psalm* 90 (89):4	O my God, You surpassed all my expectation. I want only to sing of Your mercies. "You have taught me from my youth, O God, and until now I will declare Your wonderful works. And until old age and grey hairs, O God, forsake me not." What will this old age be for me? It seems this could be right now, for two thousands years ar not more in the Lord's eyes than are twenty years, than even a single day. *SS* p. 208

The tax-collector, standing far off, would not even look up to heaven, but was beating his breast and saying, "God, be merciful to me, a sinner!" *Luke* 18:13	Your child, O Lord, has understood Your divine light, and she begs pardon for her brothers. She is resigned to eat the bread of sorrow as long as You desire it; she does not wish to rise up from this table filled with bitterness at which poor sinners are eating until the day set by You. Can she not say in her name and in the name of her brothers, *"Have pity on us, O Lord, for we are poor sinners!"* *SS* p. 212
Blessed be the Lord, my rock, who trains my hands for war, and my fingers for battle; my rock and my fortress, my stronghold and my deliverer, my shield, in whom I take refuge, who subdues the peoples under me. *Psalm* 144 (143):1-2	Oh! no, I do not have any fears of a long life and I do not refuse the fight, for the Lord is the Rock to which I am raised. *"He teaches my hands to fight, and my fingers to make war. He is my protector, and I have hoped in him."* *SS* p. 215
Jesus said "'You shall love the Lord your God with all your heart, and with all your soul, and with all your mind." This is the greatest and first commandment. And a second is like it: "You shall love your neighbour as yourself."' *Matthew* 22:37-39 'Not everyone who says to me, "Lord, Lord", will enter the kingdom of heaven, but only one who does the will of my Father in heaven.' *Matthew* 7:21 'I give you a new commandment, that you love one another. Just as I have loved you, you also should love one another. By this everyone will know that you are my disciples, if you have love for one another.' *John* 13:34-35	This year, dear Mother, God has given me the grace to understand what charity is; I understood it before, it is true, but in an imperfect way. I had never fathomed the meaning of these words of Jesus: *"The second commandment is LIKE the first: You shall love your neighbour as yourself."* I applied myself especially to *loving God*, and it is in loving Him that I understood my love was not to be expressed only in words, for: *"It is not those who say: 'Lord, Lord!' who will enter the kingdom of heaven, but those who do the will of my Father in heaven."* Jesus has revealed this will several times or I should say on almost every page of His Gospel. But at the Last Supper, when He knew the hearts of His disciples were burning with a more ardent love for Him who had just given Himself to them in the unspeakable mystery of His Eucharist, this sweet Saviour wished to give them *a new commandment.* He said to them with inexpressible tenderness: *"A new commandment I give you that you love one another: THAT AS I HAVE LOVED YOU, YOU ALSO LOVE ONE ANOTHER. By this will all men know that you are my disciples, if you have love for one another."* *SS* p. 219

You have heard that it was said, "An eye for an eye and a tooth for a tooth." But I say to you, Do not resist an evildoer. But if anyone strikes you on the right cheek, turn the other also; and if anyone wants to sue you and take your coat, give your cloak as well; and if anyone forces you to go one mile, go also the second mile. Give to everyone who begs from you, and do not refuse anyone who wants to borrow from you. *Matthew* 5:38-41 Give to everyone who begs from you; and if anyone takes away your goods, do not ask for them again. *Luke* 6:30	The poor in spirit follow Jesus' counsel: "*If anyone take away your coat, let go your cloak also.*" To give up one's cloak is, it seems to me, renouncing one's ultimate rights; it is considering oneself as the servant and the slave of others. When one has left his cloak, it is much easier to walk, to run, and Jesus adds: "*And whoever forces you to go one mile, go two more with him.*" Thus it is not enough to give to *everyone who asks*; I must even anticipate their desires, appear to be very much obliged and honoured to render service, and if anyone takes something which is for my use, I must not appear to be sorry about this but happy at being *relieved* of it. Dear Mother, I am very far from practicing what I understand, and still the desire alone I have of doing it gives me peace. *SS* pp. 226-27
All who are led by the Spirit of God are children of God. For you did not receive a spirit of slavery to fall back into fear, but you have received a spirit of adoption. When we cry, 'Abba! Father!' it is that very Spirit bearing witness with our spirit that we are children of God... *Romans* 8:14-16	If it happens that I think or say something which is pleasing to my Sisters, I find it very natural that they take it as a good that belongs to them. This thought belongs to the Holy Spirit and not to me since St. Paul says we cannot, without the Spirit of Love, give the name of "*Father*" to our Father in heaven., He is therefore free to use me to give a good thought to a soul. *SS* p. 234
Again, truly I tell you, if two of you agree on earth about anything you ask, it will be done for you by my Father in heaven. For where two or three are gathered in my name, I am there among them. *Matthew* 18:19-20	I love very much these prayers said in common, for Jesus has promised *to be in the midst of those who gather together in His name.* I feel then that the fervour of my Sisters makes up for my lack of fervour. *SS* p. 242

Rejoice with those who rejoice, weep with those who weep. *Romans* 12:15 Very truly, I tell you, you will weep and mourn, but the world will rejoice; you will have pain, but your pain will turn into joy. *John* 16:20 Each of you must give as you have made up your mind, not reluctantly or under compulsion, for God loves a cheerful giver. *2 Corinthians* 9:7	What banquet could a Carmelite offer her Sisters except a spiritual banquet of loving and joyful charity? As far as I am concerned, I know no other and I want to imitate St. Paul who *rejoiced with those who rejoice*; it is true he wept with the afflicted and tears must sometimes appear in the feast I wish to serve, but I shall always try *to change these tears into joy*, since the *Lord loves a cheerful giver*. *SS* pp. 246-47
Ask, and it will be given to you; search, and you will find; knock, and the door will be opened for you. For everyone who asks receives, and everyone who searches finds, and for everyone who knocks, the door will be opened. *Matthew* 7:7-8 Very truly, I tell you, if you ask anything of the Father in my name, he will give it to you. *John* 16:23 Let him kiss me with the kisses of his mouth! For your love is better than wine, your anointing oils are fragrant, your name is perfume poured out; therefore the maidens love you. Draw me after you, let us make haste. *Song of Songs* 1:2-4	Through beautiful parables, and often even without using this means so well known to the people, Jesus teaches us that it is enough to knock and it will be opened, to seek in order to find, and to hold out one's hand humbly to receive what is asked for. He also says that everything we ask the *Father in His name*, He will grant it. No doubt, it is because of this teaching that the Holy Spirit, before Jesus' birth, dictated this prophetic prayer: *"Draw me, we shall run."* *SS* p. 257

Thérèse (centre background) and her Carmelite sisters gathering hay, July 1896.

From Thérèse of Lisieux, *Her Last Conversations*	
Come to me, all you that are weary and are carrying heavy burdens, and I will give you rest. Take my yoke upon you, and learn from me; for I am gentle and humble in heart, and you will find rest for your souls. For my yoke is easy, and my burden is light. *Matthew* 11:28-30	As for me, with the exception of the Gospels, I no longer find anything in books. The Gospels are enough. I listen with delight to these words of Jesus which tells me all I must do: 'Learn of me for I am meek and humble of heart'; then I'm at peace, according to His sweet promise: 'and you will find rest for your souls.' *LC* p. 44
When you have done all that you were ordered to do, say, "We are worthless slaves; we have done only what we ought to have done!" *Luke* 17:10	Even if I had accomplished all the works of St. Paul, I would still believe myself to be a 'useless servant.' But it is precisely this that makes up my joy, for having nothing, I shall receive everything from God. *LC* p. 67
Mary treasured all these words and pondered them in her heart... Jesus' mother treasured all these things in her heart. *Luke* 2:19, 51	The Blessed Virgin did well to keep all these things in her 'little' heart... They can't be angry with me for doing as she did. *LC* p. 80
God will wipe every tear from their eyes. Death will be no more; mourning and crying and pain will be no more, for the first things have passed away. *Revelation* 21:4	Oh, certainly, I shall cry when I see God! No, we can't cry in heaven. Yes, we can, since it is said: 'And God will wipe away every tear from their eyes.' *LC* p. 81
So we rebuilt the wall, and all the wall was joined together to half its height; for the people had a mind to work... And each of the builders had his sword strapped at his side while he built. *Nehemiah* 4:6, 18	I read how the Israelites built the walls of Jerusalem, working with one hand and holding a sword in the other. This is what we must do: never give ourselves over entirely to our tasks. *LC* p. 96
Pilate asked Jesus, 'So you are a king?' Jesus answered, 'You say that I am a king. For this I was born, and for this I came into the world, to testify to the truth. Everyone who belongs to the truth listens to my voice.' Pilate asked him, 'What is truth?' *John* 18:37-38	I've never acted like Pilate, who refused to listen to the truth. I've always said to God: O my God, I really want to listen to You; I beg You to answer me when I say humbly: What is truth? Make me see things as they really are. Let nothing cause me to be deceived. *LC* p. 105
I am gone like a shadow at evening; I am shaken off like a locust. *Psalm* 109 (108):23	David says in the psalms: 'I'm like the grasshopper which continually changes its place.' As for myself, I can't say the same thing! I would like to walk, but my feet are tied with a rope! *LC* p. 133

Now Peter was sitting outside in the courtyard. A servant-girl came to him and said, 'You also were with Jesus the Galilean.' But he denied it before all of them, saying, 'I do not know what you are talking about.' ... After a little while the bystanders came up and said to Peter, 'Certainly you are also one of them, for your accent betrays you.' Then he began to curse, and he swore an oath, 'I do not know the man!' At that moment the cock crowed. Then Peter remembered what Jesus had said: 'Before the cock crows, you will deny me three times.' And he went out and wept bitterly. *Matthew* 26:69-75	Look at little children: they never stop breaking things, tearing things, falling down, and they do this even while loving their parents very, very much. When I fall in this way, it makes me realise my nothingness more, and I say to myself: What would I do, and what would I become, if I were to rely upon my own strength? I understand very well why St. Peter fell. Poor Peter, he was relying upon himself instead of relying only upon God's strength... I'm very sure that if St. Peter had said humbly to Jesus: 'Give me the grace, I beg you, to follow You even to death,' he would have received it immediately. *LC* p. 140
Where your treasure is, there your heart will be also. *Matthew* 6:21	You will be able to say of me: 'It wasn't in this world that she lived but in heaven, there where her treasure was'. *LC* p. 148
Then the king will say to those at his right hand, "Come, you that are blessed by my Father, inherit the kingdom prepared for you from the foundation of the world; for I was hungry and you gave me food, I was thirsty and you gave me something to drink, I was a stranger and you welcomed me, I was naked and you gave me clothing, I was sick and you took care of me, I was in prison and you visited me." *Matthew* 25:34-36	Oh! How I wish I had been infirmarian [in the Carmelite monastery], not by natural inclination but 'through the attraction of grace'... Yes, I would have had an inclination for all that. And I'd have put so much love into the work, thinking of God's words: 'I was sick and you visited me.' *LC* p. 156

Thérèse (fourth from left) and her Carmelite sisters doing laundry, 1895.

Jesus said to them [Mary and Joseph], 'Why were you searching for me? Did you not know that I must be in my Father's house? But they did not understand what he said to them. *Luke* 2: 49-50 And the child's father and mother were amazed at what was being said about him. *Luke* 2: 33	How I would have loved to be a priest in order to preach about the Blessed Virgin! One sermon would be sufficient to say everything I think about this subject... For a sermon on the Blessed Virgin to please me and do me any good, I must see her real life, not her imagined life. I'm sure that her real life was very simple. They show her to us as unapproachable, but they should present her as imitable, bring out her virtues, saying that she lived by faith just live ourselves, giving proofs of this from the Gospel, where we read: 'And they did not understand the words which He spoke to them.' And that other no less mysterious statement: 'His father and mother marvelled at what was said about him.' This admiration presupposes a certain surprise, don't you think? *LC* p. 161
We do not want you to be uninformed, brothers and sisters, about those who have died, so that you may not grieve as others do who have no hope. *1 Thessalonians* 4:13	When we are around the sick, we must be cheerful. After all, we mustn't lament like those who have no hope. *LC* p. 191
In the year that King Uzziah died, I saw the Lord sitting on a throne, high and lofty; and the hem of his robe filled the temple. Seraphs were in attendance above him; each had six wings: with two they covered their faces, and with two they covered their feet, and with two they flew. *Isaiah* 6:1-2	If I go among the Seraphim, I *shall not do* as they do! All of them cover themselves with their wings before God; I will be very careful not to cover myself with my wings. *LC* p. 198
For the lowliest may be pardoned in mercy, but the mighty will be mightily tested. For the Lord of all will not stand in awe of anyone, or show deference to greatness; because he himself made both small and great, and he takes thought for all alike. *Wisdom* 6:6-7 From the heavens you uttered judgement; the earth feared and was still when God rose up to establish judgement, to save all the oppressed of the earth. *Psalm* 76 (75):8-9	As far as little ones are concerned, they will be judged with great gentleness. And one can remain little, even in the most formidable offices, even when living for a long time. If I were to die at the age of eighty, if I were in China, anywhere, I would still die, I feel, as little as I am today. And it is written: 'At the end, the Lord will rise up to save the gentle and the humble of the earth.' It doesn't say 'to judge,' but 'to save.' *LC* p. 199

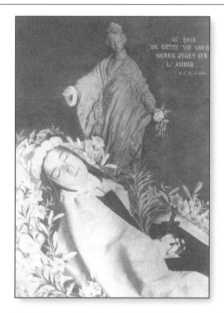

Saint Thérèse on her deathbed, 1ˢᵗ October 1897.

Pilgrims venerating the relics of St. Thérèse.

The Contributors

Johan Bergström-Allen, T.O.C. is a member of the Carmelite Third Order Secular, and is involved in the initial and ongoing formation of members of the Carmelite Family, particularly through the Carmelite Institute of Britain & Ireland (CIBI) on whose Executive Board he serves. He runs the Projects & Publications Office of the British Province of Carmelites, based in the city of York, where he is co-convenor of a Carmelite Spirituality Group. He has a particular interest in the literature of the Carmelite Order in medieval England.

Joseph Chalmers, O.Carm. was born in Glasgow, Scotland, in 1952. Having been Prior Provincial of the British Province of Carmelites, he served as Prior General of the Carmelite Order between 1995 and 2007. Renowned internationally as an exponent of Carmelite spirituality, he has published numerous books including *In Allegiance to Jesus Christ*, *Mary the Contemplative*, and *The Sound of Silence*. He has promoted the life and message of St. Thérèse through the *Little Flower Society*, and served on the national organising committee for the visit of her relics to England and Wales in 2009.

Hugh Clarke, O.Carm. (†) was ordained a priest in the English Archdiocese of Southwark in 1945 before joining the Carmelite Order some twenty years later. In a variety of roles he promoted the 'Little Way' of Saint Thérèse through his publications and the organisation of pilgrimages to Lisieux. He died in 2007.

Camilo Maccise, O.C.D. was Prepositus General of the Discalced Carmelite Order (1991-2003) and President of the Union of Superiors General for six years until 2000. During his time as senior brother of the Discalced (Teresian) Carmelites he oversaw many initiatives, including closer collaboration with the Ancient Observance of the Carmelite Order. Widely sought after as a speaker and writer, he now ministers in his native Mexico.

James McCaffrey, O.C.D. has served as Prior of the Discalced Carmelite Priory and Retreat Centre at Boars Hill near Oxford, as well as being editor of *Mount Carmel: A Review of the Spiritual Life* and of the Teresian Press. A scripture scholar who completed a doctorate at the Pontifical Biblical Institute in Rome, he gives retreats and writes extensively on the link between the Bible and Carmelite spirituality, most recently in his publications *The Carmelite Charism: Exploring the Biblical Roots* and *Captive Flames: A Biblical Reading of the*

Carmelite Saints. In 1998 he published *The Fire of Love: Praying with Thérèse of Lisieux*, and in 2008 *Prayer: The Heart of the Gospels*.

Wilfrid McGreal, O.Carm. was elected Prior Provincial of the British Province of Carmelites in 2008, having previously been Prior of the Carmelite friaries at Aylesford and Faversham in the English county of Kent. A regular broadcaster on television and radio, he has written several books including *Praying in the Carmelite Spirit*, *At the Fountain of Elijah*, and *Friar Beyond the Pale*. Serving as an Ecumenical Canon of Rochester Cathedral, Fr. Wilfrid works tirelessly to promote the unity of Christians.

Christopher O'Donnell, O.Carm. is a Carmelite friar of the Irish Province of Carmelites. Professor emeritus of the Milltown Institute in Dublin, he has published widely in the realms of Ecclesiology and Mariology, and has a particular interest in Thérèse of Lisieux, having written the highly acclaimed study of her life and message *Love in the Heart of the Church* (1997) and *Prayer: Insights from St. Thérèse of Lisieux* (2001). Together with educationalist Sr. Jude Groden, RSM, he has published several Scriptural resource books for schools and parishes.

Alexander Vella, O.Carm. has served as Prior Provincial of the Maltese Province of Carmelites, where he has been instrumental in establishing the Carmelite Institute of Malta. An expert in nurturing Carmelite spirituality, he has served on the International Formation Commission of the Carmelite Order. Following postgraduate studies at the Pontifical Biblical Institute in Rome, he spent six months in the Holy Land undertaking research which included an archaeological dig on Mount Carmel. As a member of the Malta Bible Society he worked on the revision of the Maltese translation of the Holy Scriptures.

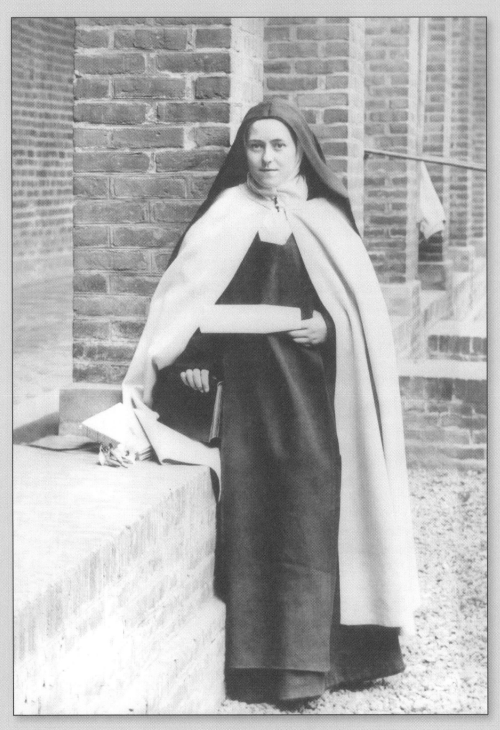

Saint Thérèse in the cloister courtyard of Lisieux Carmel on 17th March 1896.

Some recent resources on St. Thérèse of Lisieux and Carmelite spirituality

Thérèse in her own words

Story of a Soul, (trans.) John Clarke (Washington D.C.: I.C.S. Publications, third edition 1996).

Story of a Soul (study edition prepared by Marc Foley), (Washington D.C.: I.C.S. Publications, 2005).

Letters of St. Thérèse of Lisieux, (trans.) John Clarke, 2 volumes, (Washington D.C.: I.C.S. Publications, 1982-88).

St. Thérèse of Lisieux – Her Last Conversations, (trans.) John Clarke, (Washington D.C.: I.C.S. Publications, 1977).

The Poetry of Saint Thérèse of Lisieux, trans. Donald Kinney, O.C.D., (Washington, D.C.: I.C.S. Publications, 1996).

The Prayers of Saint Thérèse of Lisieux, trans. Aletheia Kane, O.C.D., (Washington, D.C.: I.C.S. Publications, 1997).

The Little Way of St. Thérèse of Lisieux from the Saint's own writings, (London: Catholic Truth Society, 1932, reprinted 2005).

A Thérèse of Lisieux Prayer Book, (Oxford: Family Publications, 2008).

Books about Thérèse

Bernard Bro, *The Little Way – The Spirituality of Thérèse of Lisieux*, (London: Darton, Longman & Todd, 1997).

Jean Chalon, *Thérèse of Lisieux – A Life of Love*, (Tunbridge Wells: Burns & Oates, 1997).

Hugh Clarke, *Message of Love – Reflections on the life of St. Thérèse*, (Faversham: Carmelite Press, 1976).

Brother Craig, *Thérèse – Teacher of Prayer*, (London: Catholic Truth Society, 2008).

Pierre Descouvement, *Thérèse and Lisieux*, (Veritas / Eerdmans, 1996).

Ida Friederike Görres, *The Hidden Face*, (San Francisco: Ignatius Press, 2003).

Guy Gaucher, *The Story of a Life: St. Thérèse of Lisieux*, (London: HarperCollins, 1987).

Jacques Gauthier, *Conversations with Thérèse of Lisieux*, (Ottawa: Novalis, 2001).

Audrey Healy & Eugene McCaffrey, *St. Thérèse in Ireland: Official Diary of the Irish Visit, April-July 2001*, (Dublin: Columba Press, 2001).

John Paul II, *Thérèse of Lisieux - Doctor of the Universal Church* (Apostolic Letter), (Strasbourg: Éditions du Signe, 1998).

Vernon Johnson, *The Message of St. Thérèse of Lisieux*, (London: Catholic Truth Society, reprinted 1997).

John Kirvan, *Simply Surrender (based on the Little Way of Thérèse of Lisieux)*, (Notre Dame, Indiana: Ave Maria Press, 1996).

Marie-Eugène of the Child Jesus, *Under the Torrent of His Love: Thérèse of Lisieux, a Spiritual Genius*, (New York: Alba House, 1995)

Eugene McCaffrey, *Heart of Love - Saint Thérèse of Lisieux*, (Dublin: Veritas, 1998).

Eugene McCaffrey, *Song of Youth: Thérèse of Lisieux, Forever Young*, (Dublin: Avila Carmelite Centre, undated).

James McCaffrey, *The Fire of Love: Praying with Thérèse of Lisieux* (Norwich: Canterbury Press, 1998).

Conrad de Meester, *With Empty Hands: The Message of Thérèse of Lisieux*, (London: Burns and Oates, 1987).

Don Mullan, *A Gift of Roses: Memories of the Visit to Ireland of St. Thérèse*, (Dublin: Wolfhound, 2001).

Thomas R. Nevin, *Thérèse of Lisieux - God's Gentle Warrior*, (Oxford: Oxford University Press, 2006).

Christopher O'Donnell, *Love in the heart of the Church - The Mission of Thérèse of Lisieux*, (Dublin: Veritas, 1997).

Christopher O'Donnell, *Prayer: Insights from St. Thérèse of Lisieux*, (Dublin: Veritas, 2001).

Thérèse of Lisieux - Living Justice, (Notre Dame, Indiana: Ave Maria Press, 2005).

Books about Thérèse's relationships with others

Patrick Ahern, *Maurice and Thérèse: The Story of a Love*, (London: Darton, Longman & Todd, 2001).

Hans Urs Von Balthasar, *Two Sisters in the Spirit - Thérèse of Lisieux and Elizabeth of the Trinity*, (San Francisco: Ignatius Press, 1992).

Marie Baudouin-Croix, *A Difficult Life - Léonie Martin, the sister of St. Thérèse of Lisieux*, (Dublin: Veritas, 1993).

Mary Frances Coady, *The Hidden Way: The Life and Influence of Almire Pichon*, (London: D.L.T., 1999).

Pierre Descouvemont, *Thérèse of Lisieux and Marie of the Trinity - the transformative relationship of St. Thérèse of Lisieux and her novice, Sister Marie of the Trinity*, (New York: Alba House, 1997).

Christine Frost, *The Parents of Thérèse of Lisieux - Were they saints?*, (London: Catholic Truth Society, 1992).

Guy Gaucher, *John and Thérèse - Flames of Love: The Influence of St. John of the Cross in the Life and Writings of St. Thérèse of Lisieux*, (New York: Alba House, 2000).

Jacques Gauthier, *I Thirst - Saint Thérèse of Lisieux and Mother Teresa of Calcutta*, (New York: Alba House, 2005).

Dwight Longenecker, *St. Benedict and St. Thérèse - The Little Rule and the Little Way*, (Leominster: Gracewing, 2002).

Christopher O'Mahony, *St. Thérèse of Lisieux by those who knew her*, (Dublin: Veritas, 1975).

Stephane-Joseph Piat, *Céline - Sister Genevieve of the Holy Face - Sister and Witness to St. Thérèse of the Child Jesus*, (Fort Collins, Colorado: Ignatius Press, 1997).

Paulinus Redmon, *Louis and Zélie Martin: The Seed and the Root of the Little Flower*, (London: Quiller Press, 1995).

Other resources on Thérèse

Little Flower Society at the National Shrine of Saint Jude, Faversham, England
St. Jude's Newsletter Office, 34 Tanners Street, Faversham, Kent, ME13 7JN, United Kingdom
www.stjudeshrine.org.uk

Society of the Little Flower

United States: Society of the Little Flower, 1313 Frontage Road, Darien, Illinois, 60561, U.S.A.

Canada: Society of the Little Flower, 7021 Stanley Avenue, Niagara Falls, Ontario, L2G 7B7, Canada

United Kingdom & Ireland: Society of the Little Flower, West Suite – 2nd Floor, Barclays House, 51 Bishopric, Horsham, West Sussex, RH12 1QJ, United Kingdom

www.littleflower.org & www.littleflower.eu

St. Thérèse National Office of Ireland
Carmelite community, Terenure College, Dublin 6W, Ireland

www.sttherese.com

The Little Way Association
Magazine available from Sacred Heart House, 119 Cedars Road, Clapham Common, London, SW4 0PR.

Sicut Parvuli – *The review of the Association of Priests and Laity of St. Thérèse of the Child Jesus*, (Secretary: Mrs Mary Harvey, 68 Northdown Park Road, Cliftonville, Margate, Kent, CT9 3PT).

The Sanctuary of Saint Thérèse in Lisieux, France
33, Rue du Carmel, B.P. 62095, F-14102 Lisieux-Cedex, France

www.therese-de-lisieux.com

The National Shrine of Saint Thérèse in the United States of America
8501 Bailey Road, Darien, Illinois 60561, U.S.A.

www.saint-therese.org

The Basilica of the Little Flower
1715 N. Zarzamora, San Antonio, Texas 78201, U.S.A.

www.littleflowerbasilica.org

Thérèse of Lisieux: an internet gateway
www.thereseoflisieux.org

Resources on the Rule of Saint Albert, and the Carmelites and Scripture

Joseph Chalmers, O.Carm., 'Hearing the Word', in *Mary the Contemplative*, (Rome: Edizioni Carmelitane, 2001), pp. 35-52.

Joseph Chalmers, O.Carm., *The Sound of Silence – Listening to the Word of God with the Prophet Elijah*, (Faversham: Saint Albert's Press, 2007).

Keith J. Egan, T.O.C., & Craig E. Morrison, O.Carm., (eds.), *Master of the Sacred Page: Essays and Articles in Honor of Roland E. Murphy, O.Carm.*, (Washington D.C.: The Carmelite Institute, 1997).

John FitzGerald, O.Carm., *Backwards into the Future: Meditations on the Letter to the Hebrews*, (Faversham: Saint Albert's Press, 2005)

Evaldo Xavier Gomes, Patrick McMahon, Simon Nolan, Vincenzo Mosca (eds.), *The Carmelite Rule 1207-2007: Proceedings of the Lisieux Conference 4-7 July 2005*, Institutum Carmelitanum Textus et Studia Historica Carmelitana 28, (Rome: Edizioni Carmelitane, 2008).

James McCaffrey, O.C.D., *The Carmelite Charism: Exploring the Biblical Roots*, (Dublin: Veritas, 2004).

James McCaffrey, O.C.D., *Captive Flames: A Biblical Reading of the Carmelite Saints*, (Dublin: Veritas, 2005).

James McCaffrey, O.C.D., *Prayer: The Heart of the Gospels*, (Dublin: Columba Press, 2008).

Carlos Mesters, O.Carm., *Defenceless Flower: A New Reading of the Bible*, (London: CIIR, 1989).

Carlos Mesters, O.Carm., 'Lectio Divina' in *Horizons*, Carmelite Spiritual Directory Project volume 10, (Melbourne: Carmelite Communications, 1999).

Patrick Thomas McMahon, O.Carm., *A Pattern for Life: The Rule of Saint Albert and the Carmelite Laity*, Carmel in the World Paperbacks 14, (Rome: Edizioni Carmelitane, 2007).

Roland E. Murphy, *Experiencing Our Biblical Heritage*, (Peabody, Massachusetts: Hendrickson, 2001).

The Carmelite Family in Britain

The Carmelite Order is one of the ancient religious orders of the Roman Catholic Church. Known officially as the *Brothers of the Blessed Virgin Mary of Mount Carmel*, the Order developed from a group of hermits in thirteenth-century Israel-Palestine; priests and lay people living a contemplative life modelled on the prophet Elijah and the Virgin Mary. By the year 1214 the Carmelites had received a *Way of Life* from Saint Albert, the Latin Patriarch of Jerusalem. Carmelites first came to Britain in 1242. The hermits became an order of mendicant friars following a General Chapter held in Aylesford, Kent, in 1247. Nuns, and lay men and women have always played a major part in the life of the Order, and have had formal participation since 1452. Over centuries of development and reform, the Carmelites have continued their distinctive mission of living 'in allegiance to Jesus Christ', by forming praying communities at the service of all God's people. The heart of the Carmelite vocation is contemplation, that is, openness to and friendship with God, pondering God's will in our lives.

Like the spirituality of all the major religious orders (Benedictines, Franciscans, etc.), Carmelite spirituality is a distinct preaching of the one Christian message. Carmelites blend a life of deep prayer with active service of those around them, and this apostolate takes many different forms depending on the time and the place Carmelites find themselves in.

Over the centuries 'Carmel' has produced some of the greatest Christian thinkers, mystics, and philosophers, such as Teresa of Jesus (of Avila), John of the Cross, and Thérèse of Lisieux (three Carmelite 'Doctors of the Church'). In the twentieth century, the Carmelite Family bore witness to the Gospel in the martyrdoms of Titus Brandsma, Edith Stein, and Isidore Bakanja.

England boasted the largest Carmelite Province in the Order until its suppression at the Reformation. The British Province was re-established under the patronage of Our Lady of the Assumption in the twentieth century. There are communities of friars, sisters and lay Carmelites across England, Scotland, and Wales. Similar communities exist in Ireland, and throughout the world. The international Order of Discalced (Teresian) Carmelite friars, nuns, and laity is also present in Britain and Ireland. Members of the Carmelite and Discalced Carmelite Orders work, live, and pray together to make up the wider 'Carmelite Family', which seeks the face of the Living God in parishes, prisons, university chaplaincies, retreat centres, hospitals, workplaces, schools, publishing, research, justice and peace work, counselling, and through many other forms of ministry.

Further sources of information on Carmelite spirituality include:

John Welch, O.Carm.,
The Carmelite Way: An Ancient Path for Today's Pilgrim,
(Leominster: Gracewing, 1996).

Wilfrid McGreal, O.Carm.,
At the Fountain of Elijah: The Carmelite Tradition,
(London: Darton, Longman and Todd, 1999).

Website of the British Province of Carmelites
www.carmelite.org

Thérèse holding a rosary, 1896.

Carmel on the web

The British Province of Carmelites
www.carmelite.org

Lay Carmel in Britain
www.laycarmel.org

Aylesford Priory, Kent
www.thefriars.org.uk

National Shrine of Saint Jude, Faversham
www.stjudeshrine.org.uk

Corpus Christi Carmelite Sisters
www.corpuschristicarmelites.org

Discalced Carmelite Family in England, Scotland & Wales
www.carmelite.org.uk

Irish Province of Carmelites
www.carmelites.ie

Anglo-Irish Province of Discalced Carmelites
www.ocd.ie

Association of Discalced Carmelite Nuns in Great Britain
www.carmelnuns.org.uk

Carmelite Forum of Britain and Ireland
www.carmeliteforum.org

Carmelite Institute of Britain and Ireland
www.cibi.ie

International Carmelite Index
www.carmelites.info

The Carmelite General Curia
www.ocarm.org

CITOC – Carmelite Communications Office
www.carmelites.info/citoc

Carmelite N.G.O. at the United Nations
www.carmelitengo.org

Edizioni Carmelitane
www.carmelites.info/edizioni

Domus Carmelitana, Rome
www.domuscarmelitana.com

Also available in the Carmelite Bible Meditations series

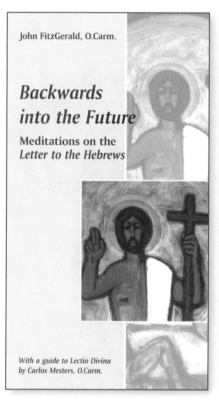

These and other titles on Carmelite spirituality
and history can be ordered from:

The Friars Bookshop
The Friars
Aylesford
Kent
ME20 7BX
United Kingdom

☎ + 44 (01622) 715770

E-mail:
bookshop@thefriars.org.uk

Saint Albert's Press
Book Distribution
Carmelite Friars
P.O. Box 140
ME20 7SJ
United Kingdom

☎ + 44 (01795) 537038

E-mail:
saintalbertspress@carmelites.org.uk

Edizioni Carmelitane
Via Sforza Pallavicini, 10
00193 Roma
Italy

E-mail:
edizioni@ocarm.org

www.carmelite.org/sap
www.carmelites.info/edizioni

The Carmelite Institute of Britain & Ireland (CIBI)

offers distance-learning courses in Carmelite spirituality, history and culture.

CIBI was established in 2005 by the British Province of Carmelites, the Irish Province of Carmelites, and the Anglo-Irish Province of Discalced Carmelites.

The purpose of the Institute is to diffuse the charism, heritage and spirituality of 'Carmel' through part-time distance-learning courses in Carmelite Studies at introductory and more advanced levels.

The Institute's scholarly but accessible programmes are open to members of the Carmelite Family and anyone interested in the field of Carmelite Studies. Through its interdisciplinary courses and activities the Institute offers an opportunity to learn about Carmelite life in its many forms, as well as a means to grow intellectually, spiritually and professionally.

CIBI's programmes – ranging from an *Adult Education Diploma* to a *Masters in Carmelite Studies* – are accredited by ecclesiastical and secular institutions of higher education, giving professional qualifications to those students who opt to submit assessments.

Thanks to the founders and sponsors of the Institute, programmes are made available to students at very reasonable rates, with a certain number of bursaries awarded to deserving individuals.

Though based in Britain and Ireland, CIBI enjoys close links with study institutes, libraries and heritage projects around the world, and welcomes student applications from any country.

For further information and a prospectus, please contact:

The Carmelite Institute of Britain & Ireland
Gort Muire Carmelite Centre
Ballinteer
Dublin 16
Ireland

☎ +353 (0)1 298 7706
Fax +353 (0)1 298 7714

E-mail: admin@cibi.ie
Website: www.cibi.ie